I0213576

Tangier 1662-80:
The First Battle Honour

Tangier 1662-80:
The First Battle Honour

The British Army in Conflict with
the Moors of Morocco

Various

LEONAUR

Tangier 1662-80: The First Battle Honour
The British Army in Conflict with
the Moors of Morocco
by Various

FIRST EDITION

Leonaur is an imprint of Oakpast Ltd

Copyright in this form © 2014 Oakpast Ltd

ISBN: 978-1-78282-409-1 (hardcover)
ISBN: 978-1-78282-410-7 (softcover)

http://www.leonaur.com

Publisher's Notes

Contents

Battle Honours for Services in the Mediterranean

By C. B. Norman

TANGIER, 1662-1680.

In the year 1910, just two centuries and a half after the event, the regiments which upheld British honour on the coast of Morocco were authorised to bear the above battle honour on their colours and appointments:

Royal Dragoons, 1662-1680. Grenadier Guards, 1680.
Coldstream Guards, 1680.   Royal Scots, 1680.
The Queen's, 1662-1680.

The King's Own Lancaster Regiment has been unaccountably omitted from this list; but there is no doubt that the 4th (King's Own), under Colonel Kirke took part in the final series of actions with the Moors prior to our evacuating the fortress.

Tangier passed into our hands, together with Bombay, as a portion of the dowry of Catherine of Braganza on her marriage with Charles II. At that time there were many who considered it the more valuable of the two acquisitions, commanding as it did the entrance to the Mediterranean. Immense sums were spent in strengthening the fortifications and in improving the harbour. The inveterate hostilities of the Moors, however, only increased with time. The one regiment first raised for the garrison, then styled the "Regiment of Tangier" (now The Queen's Royal West Surrey) was from the outset of its career engaged in a long series of engagements waged against desperate odds.

Soon it was found necessary to raise a regiment of horse to supplement the task of the infantry in dealing with the Moorish horsemen. The Royal Dragoons then came into existence, and laid the founda-

7

THE COLOURS OF THE TANGIER REGIMENT, 1684. (NOW
THE QUEEN'S ROYAL WEST SURREY REGIMENT.)

tions of that reputation for dash and discipline which has never left them. Later on, owing to the persistent hostility of the Moors, the Grenadier Guards, the Coldstreams, and the 2nd Tangier Regiment (now the 4th King's Own) were sent as reinforcements; and a reference to the Tangier Papers shows that men from the fleet were continually employed against the enemy. On one occasion Sir Cloudesley Shovel, with 600 seamen, took a leading part in the defence. Casualty returns were not so carefully prepared in the seventeenth as in the twentieth century, and I have found it impossible to discover the total losses incurred during our occupation.

Between the years 1660 and 1664 there was scarcely a month in which our troops were not fighting for their lives, and on one occasion at any rate they were so hard pressed that the governor applied, and successfully, to the Spaniards at Gibraltar for assistance. Thus it comes about that in the casualty list which has come down to us of the action on October 27, 1680, the Spanish Horse figures side by side with the Grenadier Guards.

CASUALTIES IN ACTION AT TANGIER, OCTOBER 27, 1680.

Regiments.	Officers.		Men.		Regiments.	Officers.		Men.	
	K.	W.	K.	W.		K.	W.	K.	W.
Royal Dragoons	—	2	11	35	The Queen's R.				
Grenadier Gds.	—	1	7	51	W. Surrey ..	2	10	34	120
Royal Scots ..	4	15	36	100	Spanish Horse	5	4	12	22

A few weeks after this action the King's Own (Lancaster Regiment), then commanded by Colonel Kirke, arrived as a reinforcement, and later in the year the Coldstream Guards. In 1684 the place was evacuated, having cost us many millions in money and many thousand valuable lives.

J Oliver Fe.

The Upper Castle 2 Yorke Castle   The South East corner of Tangier 1680   5 Point of Gibralter ;
2 The Mole   4 Coast of Spaine   6 The Bay of Tangier ;

History of the British Standing Army
By Clifford Walton

RISE OF THE STANDING ARMY: A.D. 1660-65

About ten o'clock on the morning of Saint Valentine's day in the year 1661, there was to be seen on Tower-Hill an ordinary London crowd collected around a small body of soldiers,—only some hundred and seventy troopers, and nine hundred or a thousand infantry. The spectacle was neither very extensive nor very imposing; yet to us who can look back upon it and upon the stream of results which has flowed from it down the long page of our country's history, it is an event of the highest military and historical interest.

That small body of men was, in its past and future, representative of two of the most patriotic and victorious armies known to history; it was the link betwixt the monarchical England of the middle ages and the constitutional England of modem times. It was, as it were, the Noah of the British Army: for it was the sole surviving remnant of that invincible host of Puritan republicans which had been swept away before the returning tide of loyalty; and it was at the same time the stock from which has sprung that British Standing Army, which has for two centuries and more been so accustomed to victory as to regard it as its inalienable right, and which has made its sovereign the ruler of near a quarter of the globe. That little band on Tower-Hill in 1661 was the seed whence has sprung England's magnificent Standing Army of the 20th century and beyond.

Very soon after ten o'clock [1] there arrived on the Hill one of the lumbering coaches of the time, and from it descended four commissioners.[2] These gentlemen, having assembled the troops around them, proceeded to inform their respective groups that they were com-

---

1. *Kingdom's Intelligencer*, 18/25 February, 1661.
2. Sir Wm. Doyle; Mr. W. Prynne; Col. Edward King; and Col. J. Birch.

missioned by King Charles the Second to congratulate the soldiers upon having been instrumental under General Monck in the king's restoration to the throne, to promise them all arrears of pay, and to enlist them into His Majesty's own service. The speeches being ended, the troops shouted "God save King Charles the Second"; the drums beat; the colours were unfurled and waved; and, in accordance with the then independent fashion of military rejoicing, the soldiers threw their hats into the air, and fired their muskets at random[3] until they were ordered to cease.

The commissaries present then took the muster, and the troops were disbanded, each man laying down his arms. Immediately afterwards they were reenlisted; and, resuming their arms, they became—from the "Lord General's Regiment of Foot,"[4] and the "Lord General's Life-Guard of Horse,"—the "Lord General's Regiment of Foot-Guards," and the "Lord General's Troop of Guards." Both these regiments were a portion of that army [5] which had lately marched from Scotland under General Monck; and the king, in consideration of Monck's instrumentality in restoring him to the throne, and glad of any excuse to retain troops in his own pay, had thus complimented the Lord General by transferring his two personal regiments to the Royal Service, at the same time appointing Monck himself "Captain-General and Commander-in-Chief"[6]

When General Monck marched from Scotland he made his last halt at the border town of Coldstream, and from this circumstance his army[7] during its progress southwards was known as the "Coldstreamers." When Monck's regiment of Foot was received into the King's service, it monopolised this sobriquet, and to this day it preserves it in its appellation of the *Coldstream* Guards.[8]

---

3. In *London Gazette*, 5 Sept., 1695, is an account of the rejoicings at Portsmouth for the taking of Namur, when the regiments in garrison were "drawn out on the parade, where they gave several volleys of *small shot*, the pikemen burning wisps of straw on the spears of their pikes, which they set fire to one after another";—evidently the pikemen's mode of a *feu de joie.*

4. Gumble: "Many thought that the general would not willingly part with his Coldstreamers . . . . However, upon Venner's insurrection, then his own regt. of Foot, with one other newly raised by H.M., were established the King's Guards; besides his Guards of Horse."

5. Gumble: *Life of Monck,* 1671.

6. *The Original Commission,* 3 Augt., 1660.

7. Gumble: *Life of Monck.*

8. In brief, this regiment was termed indifferently "The Coldstreamers," "The Coldstreams," "the Coldstream Regt.," and "The Coldstream, (continued next page),

It has been generally stated that it was not until after the death of the Duke of Albemarle (General Monck) in 1670 that the Coldstreamers were recognised as the Second or "Coldstream" Regiment of Foot-Guards"[9]; but there is reason to doubt the accuracy of this statement, although there is some colour given to it by a memorandum of James the Second's. There are extant Commissions signed by Monck as early as 1663,[10] to "my own Regiment of His Majesy's Foot-Guards"; and there are commissions of about the same period signed by the Secretary of State on behalf of the king[11] to "the Lord-General's Regiment of Foot-Guards."

At the same time in Monck's commissions [12] his regiment is more frequently styled "my own regiment of Foot."

The probability is that there existed a certain natural jealousy between this old Republican corps and the Royalist regiment of Foot-Guards,[13] and that the latter disputed the rights of the Coldstreamers to the title which itself had acquired by its attendance on the king during the Civil war; so that upon Monck's death it became requisite to definitely settle the point James the Second writes:[14]

> But so it was, that upon the general's death, his regiment of Foot, called the Coldstream, was given to Lord Craven, and made a second regiment of Guards.

Although the Coldstreamers were thus the first regiment of Foot enlisted into the Standing Army, there already existed another regiment possessing an unchallenged claim to priority. The number of Englishmen, who, urged by sentiments of loyalty, by necessity, or by love of adventure, had followed the Stuarts into exile, was considerable: and, a year or two before the Restoration, when Charles the Second and his brother James Duke of York were in alliance with the

---

regt. of Foot-Guards." It may be taken, therefore, that while it is not correct to speak of the "Coldstreams," it is absolutely correct to speak of the regiment as "The Coldstream regiment," "The Coldstream-Guards," or "The Coldstream," or "The Coldstreamers."

9. See Mackinnon's *Coldstream Guards*.

10. Commissions, 6 July, 1663, and 24 Decr., 1666, to Ensign Cox and Lieut. Stringer; W.O. Records.

11. Commission, 21 July, 1665, to Lt.-Colonel James Smith; Charles Rex and countersigned Arlington; W.O. records.

12. Various Commissions, 1665 upwards; W.O. records.

13. After Monck's death the regt. is invariably officially styled "Foot-Guards," even in the Order for Monck's funeral, which took place three months after his death.

14. *Autobiog. James II.*

Spaniards (then warring against the French in the Netherlands) these refugees had been formed by the duke into six corps.[15] On the return of Charles to England these several corps were amalgamated and sent under Lord Wentworth to garrison Dunquerque. A sort of second battalion of the same regiment, (see note following), was raised in England after the Restoration, the one battalion being denominated Lord Russell's, and the other Lord Wentworth's regiment of Foot-Guards. In 1665 the two were fused into one strong regiment of twenty-four companies. And thus, as the King's own Guards, or *First Foot-Guards*, (see note following), this regiment took precedence, as it still does, of the Lord General's or Coldstream regiment.

★★★★★★

Note:—*James II, Autobiog.* The account given by James of the origin of Lord Russell's battalion, which more truly represented the present First Foot-Guards than the other, is as follows: An insurrection by a small body of fanatics, under the leadership of one Venner, having taken place, James, then Duke of York, proposed to the Council that they should write to His Majesty and desire him to stop the disbanding of the general's troop of Horse Guards and the regiment of Foot which were to have been paid off that day, and that he would rather think of raising more men for the security of his person and government; which advice His Majesty followed, and immediately gave order for the raising a new regiment of Guards of twelve companies, to be commanded by Col. John Russell, and a regiment of horse of 8 troops, of which the Earl of Oxford was to be colonel; also a troop of Horse-Guards, to be commanded by my Lord Gerard. He likewise sent for the duke's troop of Guards which were then at Dunkirk."

Lord Wentworth's battalion landed in England from Dunquerque on the 16 Novr., 1663, and was then dispersed into garrisons. Est., 1663, Add. MSS. 28,082.

Abstract of His Majesty's Guards, 26 Janry., 1660, to 1 Janry., 1663; Brit. Mus., Add. MSS. 28,082, App. LXXXVII.

The first muster of the Regt. in England took place in Febry., 1660/1; *Mercorius Publicus*, 7 Febry., 1660/1.

Warrant, 28 Febry., 1665, for adding 1,200 men to Russell's Regt. of Guards to raise it to 2,400; *Dom. State papers.*

The following are notes upon the designations of this regiment:

---

15. Gwynne, Capt John; Mily. *Memoirs of; Edinr.* 1822. *James II, Autobiog.*

14

Est., 1660-63, Col. Russell's and Lord Wentworth's "Regts, of Foot."

R. Warrt., June, 1661, App. II, "His Majesty's regt. of Foot."

Quarters of the Forces, 24 March, 1670 (preserved in Mackinnon), "His Majesty's regt. of Foot"

R. Warrt., 12 Septr., 1666, App. XLII, "The Regt of Guards."

Cosmo's *Travels*, 1669; "The King's Own regt. of infantry."

Lond. Gaz., 13 May, 1669, and 30 April, 1670, "H.M.'s regt. of Foot-Guards."

Lond. Gaz., 3 May, 1669, and 2 May, 1670, "The Foot-Guards of H.M.'s regiment

Chamberlayne, 1679; "The King's regt. of Guards."

R. Warrt., 22 June, 1672, App. LXI, "Our regt. of Guards."

R. Warrt, 1 Mar., 1673, App. XLIV.; "Our own regt. of Foot-Guards."

Other Warrants subsequently to like effect.

Nathan Brooks, 1684, "The Royal Regt of Foot-Guards."

Estabt. List, 1692, Brit Mus., d., "First Regt of Guards."

Estabt. List, 1680, Harl. MSS. 6,425, "H.M.'s Own Regt of Foot-Guards."

Est. lists, 1685/89, "First Regt. of Foot-Guards," etc.

★★★★★★

The Lord General's Troop of Guards had similarly to give way to another regiment. During the late civil war a number of royalist noblemen and gentlemen had voluntarily enrolled themselves as a body-guard to the king,[16] their servants forming a second troop; and after the death of his father they followed Charles the Second to the Continent.[17] They were reformed in 1661, and became the King's Own, or First, troop, and the Duke of York's, or Second, troop of the regiments still famous as the *Lifeguards*.

For upwards of a century [18] the privates of this distinguished corps continued to be gentlemen of birth and education, and most of them

---

16. Draft of a speech by Marquis of Worcester in 1660; see Warburton's *Prince Rupert*.

17. The first muster of "H.M.'s Life-Guard of Horse" took place on 4 Febry., 1660/1; *Mercurius Publicus,* 7 Febry. and 21 Mar., 1660/1, and *Kingdom's Intelligencer*, 25 March, 1 660/1.

18. Domestic State Papers, 1661-1665; various petitions from unemployed officers and other gentlemen to be allowed to serve as troopers. Chamberlayne, 1669-79; "Reformed officers and young gentlemen of very considerable families who are thus made fit for military commands."

19. Chamberlayne, 1679.

looked to obtain commissions [19] after having served a period of cadet-ship in the ranks. Up to our own day the privates were still styled the "private gentlemen"[20] of the Life-Guards; and at the time I write they are still mustered by the title of "Mr."[21]

On the death of Monck in 1670, the Lord General's, which had been the Third troop of the Life-Guards,[22] became the Second troop, and the Duke of York's became the Third; for Monck's troop" being then made the Queen's took precedence of the Duke's by right of her precedence of him.

In 1686 a fourth troop[23] was added, and was evidently the troop up to that time borne on the Irish Establishment: Lord Dover commanded it, and Patrick Sarsfield was his lieutenant. This troop appears to have followed its officers in their adherence to James the Second, and it thus dropped out of the army list Its place on the English Establishment was taken by the Scotch troop of Guards a few years later.[24]

Venner's fanatical outbreak, which had served as the excuse for the revival of the First Troop of Guards, as well as the re-formation of Russell's Foot-Guards, was also utilised for the retention of another cavalry regiment of the Puritan Army.[25] We learn from the newspapers of the period immediately after the Restoration:

That the soldiers may see the affection that His sacred Majesty hath for the army, he hath been pleased to do them so much honour as to take that regiment that was lately Colonel Unton Crook's for his own, which is now styled the Royal Regiment.

20. The privates of the Irish troop of Life-Guards were also styled gentlemen as early as 1649.

21. Letter, 11 Novr., 1872. To the author from Paymaster 1st Life-Guards. The privates of Horse in the French Army used also to be styled "*Maîtres*"; *de Puysegur*, &c., &c.

22. *James II, Autobiog.*

23. R. Want., 22 May, 1686, constituting a fourth troop of Horse Guards, Capt Lord Dover, Lt. Patrick Sarsfield; and with a troop of Grenadiers attached; Home Office records.

24. List of Colonels of regts., 1743. See also Egerton MSS. 2,616, List of Forces. The colonels were as follows:—31 Decr., 1660, E. of Newburgh; 28 Janry., 1670, Marquis of Athol; 26 Oct., 1678, M. of Montrose; 1 May, 1684, Lord Livingstone; 31 Dec., 1688, D. of Queensberry; 25 May, 1696, D. of Argyll. Complete List of Land Forces in H.M.'s pay, 1696. Home Office records; the "Troop of Scots Guards." The "Troop of Scots Guards" appears also in a list of the English Army, 1 Apl., 1689, Home Office records.

25. *Mercurius Publicus*, 5 July, 1660.

But in December, 1660,[26] this Royal regiment was disbanded at Bath. When the Earl of Oxford's Regiment of Horse was raised two months later, only twenty days[27] elapsed between the signature of the warrant for its establishment and its first muster on the 16th of February, 1661. This expedition was doubtless owing to the ready enlistment of the scarcely broken Royal Regiment, whose late colonel accepted the command of the King's Own Troop in the new corps.

The title of the disbanded regiment was also revived in the new "Royal Regiment of Horse," sometimes styled Horse-Guards. It was clothed in blue, a colour worn by no other cavalry corps: some years later when a Dutch regiment in blue was brought to this country by William the Third,[28] Oxford's English regiment came to be distinguished from the Dutch Blues by the name of Oxford's Blues. I have myself often heard old people speak of the Horse-Guards as the "Oxford Blues," and until lately they were officially styled "The Blues." The regiment still takes precedence next to the Life-Guards as the "*Royal Horse-Guards, Blue.*"

There existed in the *Yeomen of the Guard* a corps far older than any of those yet mentioned, for it had been formed by King Henry the Seventh in 1485.[29] They:

. . . . .were wont to be two hundred and fifty men of the best quality under the gentry, and of larger stature than ordinary (for every one of them was to be six feet high).

The Grand Duke of Tuscany who travelled through England in 1669 gives the following account of this corps[30]:—

In the Hall (of Whitehall) called the Guardroom is the Guard of the Manica or sleeve yeomen consisting of two hundred and fifty very handsome men, the tallest and strongest that can be

---

26. The Intelligencer, 17 Decr., 1660.

27. Estabt of the newly-raised forces, 26 Janry., 1660/1. *Mercurius Publicus*, 21 Febry., 1660/1. *Kingdom's Intelligencer*, 18 Febry., 1660/1.

28. See Capt. Packe's carefully written historical record of the Horse Guards for further details. The W.O. records (Court-martial Bks. and Order books) style this regt. usually "Our regt. of Horse" or the "Royal regt. of Horse"; but in some instances it is called the "Regt of Horse-Guards," commanded by the E. of Oxford, *e.g.*, Order, 17 Octr., 1665, and others: in Order, 17 April, 1665, the expression is "Our Regt. of Guards commanded by" Aubrey E. of Oxford. In R. Warrt., 27 Feby., 1673-74. "Our Regt. of Horse-Guards," commanded by the E. of Oxford.

29. Chamberlayne.

30. Cosmo's *Travels*.

found in England. They are called in jest Beef-eaters, that is eaters of beef, of which a considerable portion is allowed them by the court every day. These carry an halberd when they are in London, and in the country an half pike, with a broad sword by their sides, and before the king had his body-guard, they escorted his carriage. They are dressed in a livery of red cloth made according to the ancient fashion and faced with black velvet; they wear on their back the king's cipher in embroidery that is Charles Rex, and on their breast the white and red rose, the emblem of the royal family ever since the union of the two houses of York and Lancaster. . . . . The duty of these Guards is, amongst other things, when the king eats in public (which he does three days a week) to fetch the meat from the kitchen and carry it to the table, where it is taken from them and placed before H.M. by the gentlemen in attendance. The captain of this Guard is my Lord Grandison, and the Lieutenant Thomas Howard.

The grand duke's derivation of the *sobriquet* of Beef-eaters is not the correct one; and it is in his account of the Yeomen's duties that we find the real origin of the name, which is merely an Anglicised corruption of the word "Buffetiers," that is, cupbearers or side-board-waiters. [31]

But the Yeomen of the Guard were employed, in Charles's reign as now, for court ceremonials only and no longer for warfare.[32]

Another corps had been instituted by Henry the Eighth,[33] styled the band of Gentlemen-Pensioners, but this also was merely a ceremonial corps.

During Charles the Second's reign the number of Gentlemen-Pensioners was reduced from fifty to forty,[34] their pay being fixed at £100 a year; they are described at this period as "usually Knights or gentlemen of good quality," and the Duke of Tuscany[35] speaks thus of them, "The king has another Guard, formed of fifty gentlemen, called Pensioners,[36] the greater part persons of birth and quality, who carry

31. Chamberlayne.
32. This nickname of Beef-eaters in 1685 was ironically applied to the Yeomen by a member in the House of Commons.—House of Commons Debates, 9 Novr., 1685. See Grose for ancient details respecting this corps.
33. Original Warrant, not dated, but signed by Henry VIII, cir. 1509; Cotton MSS.
34. Royal Warrant, 17 March, 1670.
35. Chamberlayne, 1669. For ancient details respecting this corps, see Grose.
36. Cosmo's *Travels*.

a sort of pole-axe in the form of a halberd, ornamented with gold, and are under the orders of a captain, who is my Lord Bellasyse, and a Lieutenant Sir John Bennet. They are obliged to attend the person of the king on all solemn occasions, such as receiving ambassadors and other public ceremonies; to accompany him from the ante-chamber to the chapel and on his return from the chapel to the ante-chamber: it is also their duty to serve H.M. as a bodyguard whenever he goes out into the city or into the country: on these occasions a party of them, well-armed, follows H.M.; and the captain of the body-guard is obliged by his office to keep close to the king's person particularly at the moment when he is mounting."

The members of this corps must now be half-pay or retired officers, but a warrant issued in 1685 [37] conferred upon the members a right to commissions in the army "preferably to all other persons whatsoever," whence it would appear that at that time the band was composed of cadets.

Neither the Yeomen of the Guard nor the Gentlemen Pensioners appear to have been, at any period, subject to martial law.

At the time of the Restoration there was in the French service a regiment of Scottish mercenaries renowned throughout Christendom, during four centuries past, for soldierly conduct, conspicuous bravery, and staunch fidelity. A year after his return to the throne, Charles the Second, using as a pretext the insurrection of some religious fanatics already mentioned, demanded of the French King that this Scotch regiment should return to the service of its own sovereign. Accordingly, the regiment, three thousand strong, was brought over to England.[38] In 1662 It returned to France, and continued to serve the French king for the next sixteen years (with the exception of two years, from 1666 to 1668). Notwithstanding this, it takes rank in the British Army from the year 1661 as the *First, or Royal, or Scots Regiment of Foot.*[39]

---

37. Royal Warrant, 10 Febry., 1684-5; see Grose.
38. Regimental records. Also in the Est. for 1672 (Add. MSS. 28,082, Brit. Mas., under date 27 July) appears a fresh establishment for "the Scotch regt."; and in the Est. for 1673 we find "the Scotch regt. going abroad again." Privy Council records, Edinburgh, July, 1673. Royal Order to recruit "Lord George Douglas's Scotts Regiment in the service of the Most Christian King." R. Warrts., 20 June and Aug., 1678, W.O. records; respecting the return to England from the service of France.
39. Landed in England, at Rye, 11 June, 1666. The regt. was said by tradition to have been the body-guard of the Scottish kings prior to its transfer to the French service, and it was said that it was for this reason that it obtained the prefix of "Royal." In the publications and official documents of this, (continued next page),

Even at this early stage there ran high in the new army an *esprit-de-corps*, a mutual jealousy, and a struggle for precedence. The Royals asserted that their corps was far senior to the Guards or the Coldstreamers, and shewed that they were nettled at not having precedence of these; and the others retorted by bestowing upon the sticklers for antiquity, whose origin was indeed placed so far back as to become somewhat mythical, the nickname of "Pontius Pilate's Guards."

Charles the Second, from the moment of his Restoration, sought to secure his throne by the acquisition of a strong permanent force. He wrongly attributed his father's downfall to the absence of a standing army,—wrongly, as was afterwards evidenced, for when James the Second violated the Constitution, his army did not uphold him, but on the contrary openly though reluctantly forsook him.

Charles had proposed to retain the republican army in the mass;[40] but Chancellor Hyde foreseeing that such a measure, at so delicate a juncture, would be calculated to irritate the nation, dissuaded the king from it: he argued that these were the troops that had executed Charles the First and overturned at their pleasure more than one government; that they too well knew their own power; and that, even if it were desirable to retain them, Parliament would never grant supplies for their maintenance. The king and the Parliament were indeed more than once, during the next twenty years, on the verge of an open rupture on the subject of standing forces. Charles had thus been fain to content himself at first with the five regiments already mentioned, but he was not the less constantly on the watch for plausible pretexts for adding fresh ones.

Such pretexts were not long lacking. Towards the end of 1661 Tangier became the property of the Crown by cession from Portugal, and King Charles asserted the need of additional troops to garrison the newly-acquired fortress. Accordingly a regiment of Foot [41] and a

period I find the regt. variously termed "H.M.'s Scotch Regt.," the "Scots Regt," and the "Royal Regiment of Foot." See *Lond. Gaz.*, June, 1666, Aug., 1672; Nathan Brooks; Chamberlayne; and Est. Lists 1672 to 1700. It used to beat "The Scotch March" (Dineley's *Memoirs*, 1679); it had a piper as the peculiarity of the regiment (Est. Lists, Harl. MSS.); and it had the Scotch emblems for its colours. R. Letter, 12 Feby., 1683-4, Home Office Records; "Our Scotch Regt. of Foot" coming from Tangier. May, 1684, "The Royal Regt of Foot." The regiment appears to have experienced a narrow escape from disbandment in 1678. In the proceedings of the House of Lords, 16 Decr., 1678, upon a bill for disbanding some of the forces, there appears in the list the Regt. of Foot of George, E. of Dumbarton.

40. Treatise on the Standing Army of England; Lond. 1697.

41. *Mercurius Publicus*, 24 Octr., 1661. *Kingdom's Intelligencer*, 28 Octr., 1661. Tangiers papers: State paper office; Establishment of the Morocco forces, 10 Octr., 1661.

strong troop of Horse were raised by the Earl of Peterborough, the majority of the men being supplied from the superabundance of Lord Wentworth's garrison of Dunkerque. The new forces were forthwith transported to Tangier,[42] and the celerity with which this was accomplished practically exhibits the small amount of training deemed requisite at that time to turn the raw recruit into an available soldier.

The infantry was denominated the "Tangier Regiment" On its return from Tangier in 1684, it was styled [43] "Our Most Dear Consort the Queen's Regiment of Foot." It is now the Second or Queen's regiment of Foot, and it still retains the crest of a Paschal Lamb. This crest was a national emblem of Portugal, and appears to have been selected as a compliment to the Queen's nationality and as a suitable insignia for the regiment bearing her name.

In 1680 three more troops of Horse were raised for service at Tangier; and in 1684 these (with some additions) were formed into a regiment; [44] the equipment was changed to that of Dragoons, and the corps was then entitled the "King's Own"[45] or "Royal" regiment of Dragoons; it still appears in the Army List as the *First Royal Dragoons*.

No further pretext for augmenting the army presented itself until the year 1665, when war was declared against the Dutch.

Nearly a century before this time the Dutch Government had enlisted into its service several independent companies of British subjects, a very large proportion of them being Scotchmen. From the

42. The first muster of the Horse took place in St. George's Fields, Southwark, on the 21st Octr., where they paraded one hundred strong; while the Foot numbered one thousand besides officers at its first muster at Putney Heath on the 14th October: *Mercurius Publicus*, 24 Octr., 1661.

43. Home Office records; "List of Officers" of the regiment, "the style of the Regt., Our Most Dear Consort the Queen's Regt. of Foot," May, 1684. It is styled "the Queen's Regt." by Nathan Brooks, 1684; but by Chamberlayne in the same year, "His Majesty's Tangier Regt." In Abstract of Forces, 1680, Add. MSS. 10,123, "The Tangier Regt." In Royal Warrant, 6 Febry., 1683-4, Appen. XVIII, the "Tanger Regt." It appears, therefore, to have obtained the title of "Queen's" only after return from Tangier. After the king's death it was called the "Queen Dowager's Regt."; Est. list, 1685, Add. MSS. 15,897; and Chamberlayne, 1687. For very full particulars respecting this regt., see the exhaustive *History of the Second Queen's Regt.*, by Col, Davis, 1887.

44. Royal Warrt, 15 July, 1680, W.O. records; Beating orders for six new troops of Horse for Tangier; of which six were disbanded on 9 Sept. of the same year.

45. Commissions to "Our Royal Regt. of Dragoons," 19 Nov., 1683; W.O. records. *James II, Autobiog.* Abstract of Forces, 1680; B. M., Add. MSS. 10,123. The Tangier troops, Capts. Coy's, Langston's, Neatby's, Mackenzie's troops of Horse at 40 each; "These were reduced into Dragoons when they came to England" (in 1684)

Battle of Reminant in 1578, where they fought "in their shirt-sleeves," down to the middle of the seventeenth century this corps had been engaged in all the wars waged in Holland in the cause of liberty. King Charles was not backward to perceive the advantage of obtaining in one complete body such a veteran regiment, and upon the rupture between England and the States he demanded the return home of all British subjects, that they might not have to bear arms against their own people.

On the arrival of the corps in this country it was naturally designated the "Holland" regiment,[46] and it still ranks next to the Queen's. It was a question whether the Holland Regiment should rank above the Queen's and the Royal Scots, and indeed at one time its Colonel seems to have anticipated its being created a regiment of Guards. Lord Chesterfield (who had previously raised an Infantry regiment in 1667) was promised the command of a regiment of Foot-Guards, and on being commissioned to the Holland Regiment in 1682 he so fully expected his regiment to be entitled accordingly, that in 1684 he writes[47] of it as "His Majesty's Holland Regiment of Guards," and he states also that the Duke of York promised him that the Holland Regiment "should take place of the two regiments coming from Tangier," namely, Kirke's (the Second Foot) and Dumbarton's (the First). But he was then given a commission omitting the word "Guards" and, about a week later, was informed that Kirke's and Dumbarton's were to take precedence of the Holland Regiment. Thereupon he resigned his commission.

The colour of the livery or facings has never been materially changed, and it is this colour that has obtained for the Third Foot the time-honoured name of *The Buffs*.

Thus then, King Charles the Second had already secured an army as strong in numbers as was that of the United States of America previous to their late civil war. Besides the three cavalry and five infantry regiments whose origin has been recorded, there were many independent or non-regimented companies and troops which were borne on the distinct establishments of England, Scotland, or Ireland. Several of these were at a later period amalgamated into the regular regiments

46. The Commission of the first Colonel on the English Est. is dated 31 May, 1665. The regt. is denominated "The Holland Regt." in all the Est. lists of the century, from that of 1668 (Brit. Mus., Add. MSS. 28,082) upwards; as well as Chamberlayne, Nathan Brooks, &c.; and in all the W.O. records (Court-Martial books, Commission, and Order books) from 1665 upwards. 47. Chesterfield's *Letters*. For fuller particulars see his letter to the Earl of Arran, 30 Jany., 1684.

on the English establishment; but until such amalgamation took place, they held no rank in the Standing Army, and could scarcely be reckoned as available beyond their own several intermediate localities.

Progress of the Army from 1666 to 1684

The army was probably the only institution connected with the government of the country in which Charles the Second took any personal interest; for, as has been already observed, upon the efficiency and fidelity of his forces he believed the security of his crown to depend. It may be owing to this, or it may be owing to the fact of the Army being so young and therefore so palpably open to improvement, that King Charles (as also his successor) displayed a promptitude in the adoption of improvements, which contrasts somewhat too favourably with the administrative procrastination of later times.

In 1661 [47] adjutants had been appointed as assistants to the majors in their then onerous duties.

The next innovation was the raising of a regiment of Dragoons in 1672.[48]

The origin of the word Dragoon is disputed. Some writers [49] have supposed that the French "*dragon*" from which or from the Spanish "*dragon*," we have our word, was a name first bestowed on this particular sort of troops on account of their rapidity of motion, and from the circumstance of the dragoon being specially employed for foraging or ravaging a country; thus suggesting a comparison with the dragon, the ferocious monster that used to figure so conspicuously in the tales and traditions of the middle ages. But this derivation appears rather forced.

It would seem far more likely that "dragon," [50] as the word used to be spelt even in English, derived itself from the weapon [50] peculiar

---

47 Royal Warrt, June, 1661. Commission to G. March as Adjutant to the Life-Guards, Jany., 1661; Domestic State Papers.

48. Royal Warrant, 2 Apr., 1672.

49. Turner, Daniel, Grose.

50. *Instructions for Musters and Arms*, &c., 1623; "The arms of a *Hargobuzier* " (*sic*) or Dragon (*sic*) which hath succeeded in the place of light horsemen (and are indeed of singular use almost in all the actions of war) the arms area good *Hargobus* (*sic*) or Dragon (*sic*) fitted with an iron work to be carried in a belt, a belt with a flask, priming-box, key,. and bullet-bag, an open head-piece with cheeks, a good buff coat with deep skirts, sword, girdle and hangers, a saddle, bridle, bit, petrell, crooper, with straps for his sack of necessaries, and a horse of less price than a *cuirassier's*." Markham, 1643 "for offensive arms they have a fair dragon," &c. In the Scotch Warrants (1678-83) dragoon is sometimes spelt "Dragonne," Scotch Try. Papers.

to dragoons and which was called a dragon, being a sort of large-bore flint-lock carbine,[51] very short in the barrel. This derivation seems natural, and it is supported, rather than upset, by the various ancient spellings of the word.[52] Thus Dragooner used to be more commonly used in English than Dragoon. Now *dragoner* is the German for dragoon, while *drache* is the German for dragon: this points to a foreign derivation in common with the English word, and to a derivation in no way associated with the idea of the fabulous animal. The name of the fire-arm from which the bearer of it thus took his appellation, is Spanish; for the Spaniards had not only the "*dragón*," but also the "*dragoncillo*." In the English official papers the weapon itself was frequently spelt "dragoone."[53]

Dragoons used to be simply mounted foot-soldiers, able to act as either infantry or cavalry as occasion might require.

Although it was not until 1672 that dragoons were first added to the Standing Army, they had been seen in this country many years before that time,[54] and there were many regiments of dragoons in the armies engaged in the Civil War of the King and Parliament.

The regiment raised in 1672 was disbanded two years later, and from that time until 1681 when the Scots Dragoons were brought on to the establishment, the army was altogether without dragoons; for the present First Dragoons (the Tangier Horse) remained equipped as Horse until 1684, in which year, on its return from Tangier, it was (as already narrated) converted into a Dragoon regiment.

The regiment of Scotch Dragoons just mentioned still ranks next to the First Dragoons and is of world-wide reputation under its appellation of The Scots Greys. Two troops of 100 each had been raised in 1678,[55] and after various additions, the several troops were in 1681

---

51. Markham.

52. Accounts of Soldiers, 1654; Dublin State Papers, Clarendon, Articles of War, 1673, Art. 52.

53. Representation (10 Feby., 1641) of the Offrs. of the Ordnance; "The Pistols, Carbines, *Dragoones*, Long pikes, Swords," &c., &c. Harl. MSS. 4,25a States of Ordnance Stores; appear—1669, "Snaphance Dragoones."; 1675 Do. do and "Match-" (*i.e.*, lock) "Dragoones."; 1687, Do. do.; 1688, Do. do.; 1690, Do. do. transferred to the Unserviceable column; and in 1691 only two remaining in store at all. In each of these years these weapons are *quite distinct from the Snaphance Musquets for dragoons,* or from the Snaphance musquets generally.

54. Proceedings of the House of Commons, 13 Apr., 1647. Accounts of soldiers, 1654; *Dublin State Papers.*

55. Warrant, 7 May, 1678; Scotch State Papers; *Autobiog. James II.*; Mackay's *Memoirs.* List of Colonels, 1743, states the date of embodiment to be 25 Novr., 1681.

amalgamated into a regiment, which in the Scotch Treasury records is often termed the "Royal Regiment of Dragoons" (of Scotland). Whether the regiment only gained its present appellation when it came to be mounted on grey horses, does not seem certain; but it appears highly probable that the name was originally due to the colour of the uniform, which was of stone-grey cloth.[56] The regiment had also short muskets or firelocks, with buckles and belts for slinging them.

The "Scots Dragoons" was brought on to the English establishment in 1688, but was allowed to date from 1681.[57]

In 1678 an entirely new arm was introduced into the Service, new, that is to say, to our Service, for we did but copy the Continental armies; this new arm was *Grenadiers*, or soldiers armed with hand-grenades, small bombs made for throwing with the hand. For duty as grenadiers a certain number of men were at first selected from each company, but almost immediately afterwards the grenadiers of each regiment were segregated into a company by themselves. And it may be as well to remark here, that throughout the seventeenth century companies of infantry other than grenadier or fusilier companies, were armed partly as musketeers, partly as pikemen; and the grenadiers, like the pikemen, were the tallest and finest men in the regiment.

At the same time that Grenadiers were thus added to the eight eldest regiments of Foot, a troop of mounted Grenadiers was also attached to each of the three troops of Life-Guards.[58]

---

56. Scotch Try. papers, 22 Mar., 1683, order to import "2,436 elnes of grey cloth for use of the regt of dragoons." In another Warrant, "stone-grey cloth." Scotch Privy Council Register, 13 Sept., 1684, "stone-grey" cloth for officers of Dalzell's regt of dragoons. Cannon's *Regimental records* state that the title of "The Royal Regiment of Scots Dragoons" was confirmed by royal warrant of 7 May, 1692. I have not seen this warrant. Letter, 27 June, 1689, Mackay to D. of Hamilton, styles the regt the "Scots Dragoons." It is in every probability of this regiment that Evelyn thus writes in 1694, the year in which the regt marched for Flanders: "Some regiments of Highland Dragoons were on their march through England; they were of large stature, well appointed and disciplined. One of them having reproached a Dutchman for cowardice in our late fight, was attacked by two Dutchmen, when with his sword he struck off the head of one, and cleft the skull of the other down to his chin." This regt. is often termed "The Royal Regt. of Dragoons" in Scotch Treasury Ests.; also so termed in Ests., 1680, in *Hist of Standing Armies*.

57. R. Wrrnt., Jas. Rex, establishing the regt on the English estabt., "from 1 Novr., in the 4th year of our reign," Harl. MSS. 4,847.

58. R. Warrts., 4, 6, 13 April, 1678; W.O. records. But in Home Office records is a Warrt, 11 July, 1683, for pouches for the use of the three troops of Grenadiers new raised for our service.

Owing to King Charles's subservience to the French interest, there were no wars of any national importance during his reign; nevertheless the army was not altogether inactive, and the few incidents of active service of interest that did occur must not be wholly passed over.

In 1672[59] the capture of the island of Tobago was effected by a body of troops which went from Barbadoes under the command of Sir Tobias Bridges.

In 1675 and 1676 troops were employed in a desultory warfare with the North American Indians in Virginia,[59] and eventually the most troublesome of the tribes were reduced to quietude. But we must turn from the bare mention of the actions of non-regimented troops to the narrative of the doings of the regiments already incorporated into the Standing Army.

In 1672, an alliance having been formed with France against Holland, war was declared with this latter country. The traditional ceremony of *Public Declaration of War* was observed on this occasion, and it is interesting to notice how closely it resembles that observed on the declaration of war with Russia in 1854. The *London Gazette*[60] thus briefly describes the ceremony in 1672:—

There met at the Court-Gate—
    The Marshall's Men.
    Ten Trumpets.
    The Sergeant-Trumpeter.
    Three Officers-of-Arms' Assistants.
    Two Heralds to proclaim.
    Three Sergeants at Arms.
    A party of the King's Troop of Guards.
The proclamation being ended, they proceeded from thence in a very regular manner to Temple Bar, where having stayed some little time, they were met by the Lord Mayor and Aldermen of the City, and at the end of Chancery Lane they made the second proclamation.

Another proclamation was made at the end of Wood-street Cheapside, and a fourth at the Royal Exchange. All the party were afterwards entertained by the Corporation, the soldiers having a table to them-

---

59. *London Gazette.*

60. *London Gazette*, 1 April, 1672; and 12 Feby., 1665, and 21 Octr., 1697. Letter, Chelsea, 6/16 March, 1665, Ambassador Van Goch to States-General describes a similar ceremony at that time; Dom. State Papers.

selves in the same hall.

For this war a British Contingent of six thousand men was made up from the First Foot (which had returned to France in 1668), from the Foot-Guards, and from the Scotch and Irish establishments. One hundred and fifty of the Life-Guards also accompanied the Contingent, and many gentlemen-volunteers were attached to it This service gave the English levies some notion of real and scientific warfare: to the officers the advantage of serving under such leaders as Condé and Turenne was invaluable, and several good soldiers were formed for us by the campaigns of this war.

Conspicuous among the number was John Churchill, captain of the grenadier company of a newly-raised regiment commanded by the Duke of Monmouth. This Captain Churchill was already pointed out as a rising man. He did not disappoint the predictions of his admirers; as the first Duke of Marlborough he became the greatest captain England had ever produced.

It has been asserted that the reasons for Churchill's rapid elevation[61] are to be found in the passion with which he inspired one of the king's mistresses, or in his sister's influence with the Duke of York. However this may be, it is certain that Churchill was from the first noted throughout the army, not so much for his court interest, as for his skill and energy as an officer and for his coolness and pluck in action.

The son of a Devonshire country clergyman [62] who had been impoverished through his loyalty, and whose reminiscences were all of the long Civil War, young Churchill's whole ambition tended towards the profession of arms, and he eagerly embraced the offer of a commission in the Guards. That the influence of his court friends was of use to him is to be reasonably presumed, but to every man come at some period of his life external aids, and the difference in men consists mainly in their degrees of fitness to take prompt advantage of such flood-tides in their affairs.

John Churchill was ambitious, and resolved that his apprenticeship should not be spent in idling. He volunteered for Tangier,[63] and

---

61. Churchill's Commissions ran thus: Ensign, 1666; Captain, 1672; Colonel, 3 Apr., 1674, and again 17 Feby., 1677/8; Brigr.-Genl., 1685; Major-General, 1 July, 1685; Lieutenant-General, 7 Novr., 1688. It will be observed that he was promoted from Ensign to Captain direct. The rapidity of some of the later promotions may be due to the great increase of the army.
62. Lediard, Coxe, Rousset and Dumont.
63. Lediard, Coxe, Rousset and Dumont.

although but a short time with the garrison of that place, he did not leave before he had attracted the notice of his comrades.

Though he was yet only a youth of two-and-twenty [64] when he accompanied the Duke of Monmouth to Holland, the great Turenne remarked his conduct, and prophesied a splendid future for him. Captain Churchill possessed the advantage of a remarkably handsome person, and he received in the French camp the sobriquet of "*le bel Anglais.*"[64]

On one occasion a French colonel abandoned a post which he had been ordered to maintain as one of extreme importance. Turenne, exasperated at the loss of the post, and desirous of at once recovering it and shaming the colonel, offered to bet a supper and wine that "*le bel Anglais*" would retake the position with one-half the number of men that lost it Churchill and his men justified the general's confidence and won his bet for him, but not without a sharp fight

Another occasion on which the English troops gained much applause was at the siege of Maestricht in 1673,[63] when young Churchill at the head of his grenadiers accompanied the storming party led by the Duke of Monmouth on the twenty-fourth of June to the attack of the counterscarp; it was he who first planted the French flag at the top of the breach. A lodgement was effected, but during the night the Dutch, under cover of the explosion of a mine, recovered the work, driving out the *Gardes Françaises* and *Gardes Suisses* who were on duty. At this critical moment the duke and Churchill, with only twelve "Gentlemen" Privates of the Lifeguards,[65] rushed to the front, passing, in order to come at the enemy, along a line of fire and within twenty yards of it; checked the enemy's further progress; and, having by their example rallied the flying troops, regained the work before the hour arrived for handing it over to the relieving guard.

The Duke of Monmouth informed his sovereign that Churchill's bravery had been the saving of his life.[66] The thanks of the French king were given to the young British grenadier at the head of the army; and

---

64. Born 24 June, 1650, at Ashe, in Devonshire.

65. The *London Gazette*, 23 June, 1673, says only that they were 12 volunteers " all of them the King of Great Britain's subjects." An account of the same action published by Thos. Newcomb, Lond. 1673, says "about a dozen English volunteers," "persons of quality." R. Warrt., 20 May, 1674, W.O. records, is for the issue of 12 carbines to 12 Gentlemen of the King's, or First, troop of the Life Guards, in lieu of 12 lost in the trenches at Maestricht, and gives the names. See also Cannon; who, however, quotes no authorities.

66. Lediard, Coxe, Rousset and Dumont.

he was strongly recommended for promotion by the French generals. At the age of twenty-three he was promoted to a colonelcy.

At this same period was being waged a war of quite a different kind; less scientific and on a smaller scale, but more trying because less civilised; not so fame-bringing, but far more harassing, and which is more intimately connected with this history than the war in Holland. On the Continent a comparative handful of Englishmen were fighting under foreign generalship, while at Tangier British soldiers under British generals were defending a British fortress against a most determined foe.

A detailed narrative of this defence is due to the valour of the distinguished regiments engaged in it

THE DEFENCE OF TANGIER: *A.D.* 1662-80.

Tangier, the scene of the earliest exploits of our Standing Army, is a sea-port town on the north coast of Morocco, and to a certain extent commands the western entrance to the Straits of Gibraltar. The Moorish sentry, as he stands or rather lolls, on his post upon the ramparts of Tangier, can take in at one glance the whole Strait. The Atlantic lies on his left; in front he can plainly distinguish the low white walls of Tarifa and all the southernmost coast of Spain; to his right rises the craggy mountain of Apes' Hill, and opposite this, and faintest of all, juts out the corpse-shaped rock of Gibraltar. Not a ship can enter the Strait at either end without being espied from Tangier.

The town is built on a slope which rises from the beach, the north-western and highest part of the acclivity being occupied by the Castle and the stronger works, the town itself being also walled about. A place of great antiquity,[67] it had passed through the hands of the Carthaginians, the Romans, the Goths, and the Moors, and had in the fifteenth century been taken by the Portuguese. The Portuguese, during their occupation of the place, were constantly annoyed by the Moors; and the marriage of their Infanta to Charles the Second in 1661 afforded a favourable opportunity of getting rid of so troublesome a property by making it over to an ally. At the time of its cession to England, Tangier, although declining in prosperity, was still a place

---

67. The original founders of the city were the Canaanites; and Procopius tells us that there were still to be seen in his time two columns in the town whereon was an inscription in the Phoenician language as follows, "We fled from the robber Joshua the son of Nun." Procopius wrote in the middle of the sixth century, two thousand years after the conquest of Canaan by the Israelites.

of some maritime importance as a harbour for Mediterranean-bound ships as well as for vessels passing from Europe towards the Cape of Good Hope and India. Probably no city in the world within the limits of civilisation has so little changed as Tangier, and the modern visitor may still see the guard-room where the men of the Second Queen's kept the Land-port gate; he may still walk along the ramparts once paced by the sentinels of Dumbarton's or the Foot-Guards; and the gate-way still stands by which the Royals used to gallop out to a skirmish with the horsemen of Omar Ben Haddn.

The very streets are but little altered, and the imagination can in a moment people them with the red-coated soldiers of Charles's reign with their matchlocks and rattling *bandaleers*: the same mongrel crowd of Jews, Genoese, Moors, Spaniards, and Levanters filled the narrow streets and the bazaars then as now, and doubtless many a wrangle took place daily in the market-place betwixt the huckstering stall-keepers and the overbearing English soldiery.

Tangier is in form quadrangular, the north-western angle being the highest ground; and from that angle and from the northern side there is a regular slope towards the south side and towards the sea on the north-eastern side. The whole city was walled in. On the north-western height was Peterborough Tower, a work of no great strength: the precipitous cliffs on which the tower stood overlooked the Atlantic, and down these cliffs a *palisado* was run from the city wall to the sea. At the top of the *palisado* and adjoining the angle of Peterborough Tower was a stout bastion from which the wall continued along the gradually-lowering heights down to the north-eastern angle, where was a landing-mole guarded by a tower and port. As the attacks of the Moors were confined to the land side of the city it is unnecessary to describe the defences on the side of the Straits.

The main defence on the land side consisted of a series of out-works so placed as to form a complete outer line of forts, within musquet shot of each other; and these were connected by ditches, and in some places by *palisadoes*, the whole being three miles in compass on the land side.

Improved as the art of war had recently become in the middle of the 17th century, the defences of Tangier were not of a nature to have withstood a serious siege by a properly equipped army of Turks, Spaniards, or Frenchmen, but they were strong enough to offer a prolonged resistance to a people so backward in civilisation as were the Moors, and to an army whose chief dependence was upon its irregular cavalry.

The military system of Morocco was a sort of feudal militia.[68] Each tribe of Arabs or each division of the country was subject to a call from its district chief or *moukadem*; there was no Standing Army,[68] and there was no Field Administration, but each man repaired to the rendezvous, upon an alarm, with his own arms and his own supplies.[69] The consequence of this disjointed state of things was that the *sultan* and his generals experienced much difficulty in organising any simultaneous action among the many semi-independent chiefs and tribes; and that when an army had at length been assembled,[68] it was impossible to maintain it long in one spot.

Without a system of supply, without transport, without artillery, without drill, the mode of Moorish warfare was entirely irregular and was infinitely better calculated for a campaign on open plains, deserts, and jungles, than for a close siege. Excellent horsemen, the Moorish cavalry felt able to cope with any foe in the open, and the foot soldiers were apt at ambushes and concealed movements, but individual courage and individual intelligence could not compensate for the advantages conferred by the European system of drill. The Moors fought without order,[68] observing neither ranks nor files; when compelled to give a pitched battle the Horse led the van and covered the rear, while the Foot composed the main body. Some of the Foot carried lances and some fire-arms.

The new owners of Tangier were not long suffered to remain undisturbed. Parties of Moors, under various independent chiefs, kept up a desultory warfare, and intermittent annoyance rather than any systematic attack. On the third of May, 1662, the Tangier Horse had a party out foraging, when the Moors came[70] down upon them: thereupon Major Fines was dispatched from the town with some six hundred men to bring in the Horse: the major was in such haste to start that many of his men had no powder in their *bandaleers*, and the result was that the whole party was cut to pieces by the Moors close to where Kendal's Fort afterwards stood.

A year after this the Earl of Teviot succeeded the Earl of Peterborough as governor; and his first act was to ratify a treaty of boundary

---

68. *The interest of Tangier*; Lond. 1680. Harl. Misc.

69. let it be observed *en passant*, that a return to a similar militia system in our own country is being at this moment (1872) advocated by many civilian members of the legislature,

70. Thacker; The English had been the aggressors from the first; *Mercurius Pub.*, 12/19 June, 1662.

with the Moorish Government. [71] But unfortunately, before another twelvemonth had elapsed, the English broke the treaty by annexing about one thousand acres of land,[71] including the site of Charles Fort. The natural sequence was a fresh outbreak of hostilities; and in the Spring the Moors made a demonstration more threatening than any yet attempted since the British occupation. The Earl of Teviot, finding that the presence of so large a body of Moorish troops rendered Tangier a prison to its garrison and cut off the supplies from the neighbouring country, resolved to attempt its dispersal.

On the first of March the Moors were seen planting a standard on an eminence at no great distance, preparatory to breaking ground against some of the outlying forts. The governor ordered out a troop of the Tangier Horse (Royal Dragoons) and, taking the captain of the troop aside, showed him the red flag of the Moors, and told him that he expected his men to bring it in. Captain Witham mounted, drew his sword, and placed himself at the head of his men. The gate was flung open, and whilst the men of the Royals and the Queen's flocked from the guard-room to the walls to view the coming fight, the Tangier Horse rode proudly out to the maiden battle of their since distinguished corps. On those sunny slopes in front of the walls of Tangier promise was given of the troopers that should capture French colours at Waterloo and ride through Russian masses at Balaklava. A most dashing onset, afterwards maintained with the greatest spirit, placed the standard in the hands of the English troopers and effectually routed the enemy.

The Moors esteemed themselves the most perfect horse-soldiers in the world; and, unwilling to confess themselves defeated by cavalry, on the thirteenth of the same month they made shew of a challenge. It was readily accepted, and again the impetuosity and determined courage of the Tangier Horse was found irresistible by these hitherto invincible centaurs. Again a few days afterwards some of the enemy surprised a party of the Tangier cavalry, but the Englishmen were still too much for them, and they were beaten.

All this time the garrison was harassed by being kept constantly on the alert, and on the fourth of May Lord Teviot planned a general sally with the view of breaking up the enemy's army. The battle was one of those hand to hand *mêlées* which have now long been unknown to civilised warfare: the struggle was fierce and protracted, and the loss to the garrison as well as to the Moors was very severe. The Earl of Teviot

---

71. Thacker.

was killed in the action. However the Moors were thoroughly beaten and the object of the fight was gained; for they drew off, and, except at rare intervals, and then to no great extent, did not interfere with the English garrison for some time.[72]

Principally owing to the difficulties that lay in the way of collecting and subsisting an army, it was fifteen years[73] ere the Moors assembled again in any force before Tangier.

There was however a man named Omar Ben Haddn, the Alcaid of Alcazar, distinguished alike for his qualities as a general and for the vehemence of his hatred to the English. Omar alone possessed the tact and resolution required to organise an united army, together with the shrewdness to plan, and the perseverance to execute, an effective siege. He was, nevertheless, in no way in advance of his countrymen in the matters of humanity and honour; being, on the contrary, more thoroughly Eastern than most Moors in his mingling of Eastern duplicity and barbarity with the courtesy of the Arab. He was already well known to the garrison of Tangier; and four years before this, in one of the desultory attacks on the garrison, when Buliph, an even more active and bitter enemy than himself, was slain, Omar Ben Haddn lost his hand by a bullet from an English musket. Omar had, since Buliph's death, conducted the occasional raids against the English, and had been on the whole more successful than his predecessors. Encouraged by these occasional negative triumphs, he obtained authority from the *sultan* to organise further operations on a grander scale; and in April, 1679, he appeared before the outlying forts of Tangier with at least five thousand foot and six hundred Horse. [74]

Less than half a mile in advance of Peterborough tower, but nearer to the sea, was Henrietta fort forming the extreme right of the English lines. A little in advance, again, of this, and close to the shore, was a building named Whitby Fort supported by a wood-built redoubt. In Whitby fort were stationed eight and twenty men under a sergeant, while another sergeant and twelve men occupied the redoubt.

Omar Ben Haddn perceived that no success against the left of the

---

72. At the time that I first wrote this chapter I had no intention of quoting my authorities as I have since done; and although I have disinterred many of them, some of those for the defence of Tangier are lost; most of the events are, however, recorded in the *London Gazettes*; and also various authorities quoted throughout this chapter.
73. Desultory attacks were however not unfrequent during this interval, especially in 1669, 1670 and 1671. *London Gazette*, 16/19 Aug., 1669; 14/18 July, 1670; July & Aug., 1671.
74. *Second journal of the Siege of Tangier*, Lond. 1680.

English lines would give him entrance to the fortress; whereas if he could once command it and thus effect an entrance into Peterborough Tower, the town and all that lay below the western height must eventually fall into his hands. He therefore wisely resolved to bend his strength against the English right, beginning with Whitby redoubts as the most advanced posts.

On the third of April the *alcaid* made a demonstration against the whole line of forts, but he privately detached a strong body to attack at Whitby under cover of the diversion thus created. The English governor, the Earl of Inchiquin, fell into the snare. The points most threatened were re-inforced and no thought was given to Whitby. But the two sergeants (whose names were worthy of preservation[75]) were equal to their commands. The larger building was a low house with a small tower at the end of it; the other was merely a log hut.[76] Both were of course loop-holed, and from within the English soldiers kept up a constant fire on the thick groups of the enemy. At length the Moors made a rush on the house, crowding in hundreds up to the very loop-holes. The Englishmen continued to fire and could not fail to hit, so thick were the enemy. Some of the Moors, however, were pushed up by their comrades on to the roof, and soon fifty or sixty of them were knocking in the roofing and firing down. The sergeant had wisely prepared for this contingency; and, withdrawing his party into the tower, he blew up the rest of the house with the men upon it.

The howls of pain were followed by yells of disappointed rage, and all the mass of the unhurt came on with fury against the tower. Bravely, nay, nobly did the little band and their spirited leader defend their weak citadel for a long hour. Man after man dropped; hope of relief from the lines gave place to certainty of death; yet still did the sergeants encourage their men, still did the soldiers stand by their sergeants. Seven men only, besides the sergeants, were left when a corner of the building gave way before the sheer weight of the crowds of Moors, and the tired Englishmen saw themselves exposed to the open attack of those whom they had so long defied. They resolved to take no quarter, for death was preferable to slavery, and they made a rush for their lives. One or two escaped, but the gallant sergeants did not live to tell the tale of their own doings.

---

75. Since writing the above, I have succeeded in discovering the name of the sergeant who commanded in the fort; for his wife Mary Heathley, received £60 Royal bounty. See also Note (1744). Guy's Schedule of secret service payments 1679-88.
76. *London Gazette.*

With not less pluck and determination was the wooden redoubt defended. Its sides were soon riddled and broken, and the enemy gathered so close to the walls that fire-arms could no longer be used. The men with their swords and half-pikes still kept at bay the Moors with their javelins and scimitars. Half of the dozen Englishmen were dead, the arms were nearly all broken to pieces, and the Moors had begun to swarm over the redoubt like bees. Then and not till then did the sergeants order his remaining comrades to try and fight their way to the Lines. He himself remained behind, determined not to abandon his post while there was yet work to do. Preparing a train he blew up the redoubt with himself and some forty of the enemy. Altogether the Moors lost some two hundred and fifty men.

The conduct of such men as these of the Royals and the Queen's (in days when there existed no such order as that of the Victoria Cross) proves that to the British soldier no incitement beyond that of duty and *esprit de corps* is required to evoke the most splendid deeds of valour.

The extraordinary bravery displayed by the two sergeants and their little following had such an effect on the Moors that the *alcaid* found it necessary to enter into a truce, in order that he might draw off until the impression created by this action had in some degree faded.

This truce was afterwards renewed, although Omar Ben Haddn was again collecting an army in the neighbourhood of the British fortress. The excuse he made for this apparent inconsistency was that the *sultan* had intelligence of an intended French landing on that coast; indeed, he alleged that this was the only reason for the extension of the truce.

On the twenty-fifth of July the treacherous Moor deliberately broke the truce, attempting a general attack on the English lines in the middle of the night. The governor of Tangier was not so entirely inexperienced in the Eastern mode of dealing, nor so unwary, as not to have taken care to maintain the line of forts and outposts in the highest state of preparation; and the Moorish soldiers, deceived in their expectations of an easy victory, and many of them with a still keen recollection of the prowess of the redcoats at Whitby, could not be induced to make a sustained attack. Several times their chiefs led them on, but come to close quarters with the Englishmen they would not. For some days the *alcaid* did his best to inspire his men with greater confidence, but the panic was too strong for him, and he had to retire.

On the third of November the crimson fez caps, the blood-red or green standards, and the white burnouses of the Moors were again espied moving towards the city. As soon as they had pitched their tents the Moors broke ground to make approaches; and on the fifth they attacked the most advanced forts, but without any success.

Omar had profited by his long experience of his enemy, and he now began to turn to account the lessons he had learned. He had noticed that in an assault, or in a hand to hand fight with even largely superior numbers, British soldiers could not be vanquished. For nearly twenty years the Moorish chiefs had trusted to overwhelming numbers and Moorish bravery, but in vain. English infantry had been found invincible in their quiet resolute firmness, whilst English troopers had again and again proved themselves more mettlesome than the vaunted Moorish cavalry. It was necessary to devise some different tactics for the subjugation of Tangier to those hitherto employed. Omar to his great delight had discovered these new means, and he now went to work methodically to form gradual approaches to the English lines. These approaches were not the trenches of modern warfare, but broad ditches [77] some eighteen feet deep, with the earth dug out, forming a high embankment on either side, in fact covered ways. The obvious intention of the enemy was to surround with a trench each fort in succession, when it must fall into his hands, provided only that any sally from the town itself could be repulsed.

Now there could be no greater obstacle to a successful sally than such deep trenches as the Moors were cutting. This mode of attack was quite new from the Moors, and surprised as well as alarmed the garrison. Lord Inchiquin foresaw that if the forts were left to themselves they must inevitably fall one by one, under this new plan of Omar's. The only way to avert such consequences would be to destroy the enemy's approaches by a succession of sallies, to throw into the forts fresh supplies as needed, and to adopt as far as possible an offensive in lieu of a defensive attitude.

The governor suffered no delay to endanger his small prospects of success, and grenadiers were at once sent to the front to annoy the enemy's working parties with hand-grenades. On the morning of the seventh Admiral Herbert landed with a Naval Brigade of three hundred and fifty men, and a considerable sally was made with great success.

The direction of the enemy's approaches was towards Charles fort;

77. *A Second Journal of the Siege of Tangier.*

and already, notwithstanding a severe check from a sally on the eighth, he had carried mines under James and Kendal Forts, the two redoubts farthest from the town. A day or two later two other redoubts had to be abandoned because they were in danger of isolation. Fortunately for the English interests the *alcaid* was anxious to get to court to boast of his exploits. He had done more than any general before him; and he deemed it well to present himself to the *sultan* before attempting more difficult tasks, and possibly failing. The English governor was not to be enticed into a truce this time, and so the Moors blew up the abandoned forts and disappeared.

Omar went up to Fez with a suitable present for the *sultan*, and with his mouth full of terrific assaults on redoubts, magnified by Eastern hyperbole into castles and fortresses. The Sultan was however better informed than the *alcaid* supposed. He received his general graciously, and accepted his present; but in the middle of Omar's bragging narrative he interrupted him by asking if he had taken Charles Fort, and upon receiving a reply in the negative, listened coldly to the rest. The crestfallen general made his obeisance and retired to arrange for a fresh attack.

On the twenty-fifth of March Omar Ben Haddn once more appeared before the white walls of Tangier with about seven thousand men.[78] He at once commenced to open trenches from Teviot Hill towards the English lines between Charles and Henrietta Forts. Lord Inchiquin promptly took measures to place these forts in the best condition for defence. A whole company of the Queen's was sent to reinforce Charles Fort, and plenty of provisions and ammunition were sent out. Breaking ground on Teviot Hill the Moors made their approaches in such a way as to cut off Henrietta Fort from Charles Fort, completely intersecting the English lines. The garrison was too weak to prevent this; but reinforcements were daily expected from home, and it was hoped that the two forts would be able to hold out until in a condition to compel the raising of the siege.

The Moors were capital navvies, and the progress they made with their trenches was extraordinary. From their main trench they dug two large trenches cutting off Henrietta Fort from Charles Fort, and so rounding Charles Fort as to sever the communication of the latter with the town. The depth of the trenches, generally as much as fifteen or eighteen feet, together with occasional blinds, rendered it extremely difficult for the men in Charles Fort to do much execution,

---

78. An *Exact Journal of the Siege of Tangier, 1680*. A *Journal of the Siege of Tangier*, 1680.

until they erected a cavalier of such a height that they could fire on the working parties at the bottom of the trenches. The annoyance was not, however, sufficient to cause any great delay in the works; and the Moors, rejoicing in the prospect of at length circumventing the Christian interlopers, exhibited their exultation by planting flags along their new trenches; the garrison of Charles Fort, however, made such good artillery practice at these that they were reluctantly withdrawn.

A branch was now made on the Henrietta side going towards the sea to cut off Henrietta fort from the town. Having in this manner succeeded in preventing any relief from the town to the forts, Omar attempted to possess himself of the thus isolated works. He commenced a mine towards Charles fort from the south side of it. With Henrietta fort he tried more speedy means. On Easter Sunday, the eleventh of April, a great pent-house called a cat or tortoise, was wheeled up to the very wall,[79] and under its shelter the Moorish soldiers began to dig a deep hole: the hole being charged with powder and well filled in again, an explosion would blow in the wall of the fort. However, the men in the fort kept up so rapid a discharge of musketry and hand-grenades that the enemy was repulsed with considerable loss before the mischief could be effected.[80] The *alcaid*, foiled in this attack, ordered a mine to be opened towards the fort.

On the twenty-ninth a Moorish flag was sent to acquaint Charles Fort that the mine was ready, and that if the English did not at once surrender it would be fired. The gallant Captain Trelawney replied that "he was placed there to maintain the fort and not to yield it, and that the enemy might do "his worst." [81] Omar sent again to say that two of the garrison might come and see the mine for themselves. Two men accordingly went out. Their report of the mine was so far reassuring to their expectant comrades that they testified their defiance of the Moors by firing volleys and rigging a rope with English flags.

Still it was a nervous moment for the two captains and their two hundred men; for so confident were the Moors of the success of their mine that they proceeded to fire it With ill-disguised anxiety the movements of the enemy were watched by the men in the fort. At length it could be guessed that all was ready. The Moors were leaving the mine, and the barbarians in anticipation of their triumph displayed all the symbols of victory. Slavery or death stared in the face those gallant men of the Sec-

---

79. *Exact Journal. Second Journal. London Gazette.* Thacker.
80. *Second Journal.*
81. *Second Journal, Exact Journal.*

ond Queen's.

Even yet there was time to hail the enemy and surrender on terms: but no, they will be true to death to the colours they still defiantly wave. The last two or three quit the mine. The Moors themselves are silent. The man entrusted to light the train runs from the dangerous spot British and barbarians are alike in suspense for a few moments longer, moments that must have seemed like ages to the devoted garrison.—A shake, a dull sound, a roar, and the mine has exploded. The exasperated Moors see the fort still standing unharmed, and, as the smoke clears off, the red cross of St. George still flying. The *alcaid* was disappointed, but not discouraged.

On the day following the failure of the mine he sent into Tangier to compliment Sir Palmes Fairborne on his arrival as governor; and to say that his life might be a long or a short one, but that he intended not to stir from the place until he had taken every fort and reduced Tangier to its old limits.

Sir Palmes Fairborne had lately arrived from home to resume the command. He had been closely followed by four companies of old soldiers of the Royals,[82] and four companies from Ireland for the same regiment; and two months later other reinforcements [83] also arrived consisting of five companies of the First and Second Foot Guards and a fresh batch of the First Foot: Lord Mulgrave, Colonel of the Third Foot, commanded the reinforcements,[84] and he was accompanied by Lord Mordaunt (afterwards the famous Earl of Peterborough), Lord Plymouth, Lord Lumley, and other noblemen as volunteers.

There were with the Moors several Europeans,—Frenchmen and Levanters. There were even one or two captives from the garrison of Tangier who had preferred to serve the *sultan* against their late comrades (perhaps with the hope of escape) rather than be sent up country into hopeless slavery. These men, to the best of their low abilities, instructed the Moors in the arts of gunnery and mining, arts still in their infancy even among the most advanced nations.

The practice of the Moors in the former was limited for want of guns, but their success in the latter elated them greatly. When they discovered that their newly-adopted plan of sapping the place they desired to reduce was regarded with anxiety if not alarm by these hitherto fearless Englishmen, their hopes rose, and they worked like

---

82. *Lond. Gazette.* Royal Warrt., 4 June, 1680 (presd. in Mackinnon).
83. Royal Warrt., 4 June, 1680, telling off the reinforcements into battalions.
84. *Lond. Gaz.*, 24/27 May, 1680.

galley slaves at their mines.[85]

They now became possessed of some more guns, probably from some ship wrecked or captured down the coast; for on the eighth of May they brought to bear on Henrietta fort two pieces,[86] the one a three, the other a six-pounder. The next day a breach appeared in the wall of the fort. Sir Palmes Fairborne signalled [87] to Omar Ben Haddn that the fort should be surrendered if the men were suffered to come into the town. "I want not stone walls but slaves,"[85] replied the Moor, well aware of the effect of every tangible trophy upon his master the *sultan*.

Both Charles Fort and Henrietta Fort had become quite untenable. In the latter there gaped a breach, and against both mines were being approached from every side.[88] A council of war was called by the governor and it was resolved to cover by a sally the evacuation of Charles Fort. It might perhaps have held out for a few days longer; but so dangerous were by this time the mines under it that the soldiers declared they would abandon it after three days, whether their officers stayed or not. [89]

On the morning of the fourteenth the guns in the fort were spiked, and all ammunition and material was piled together in readiness to be blown up. The men, at this time one hundred and seventy-six in number,[90] fell in to await the signal from the town.

The sallying party was divided into five bodies.[91] Captain Hume with a company of the First Royals was to advance straight on the enemy's trenches. Major Boynton was to command the main body of one hundred and forty men [92] to sustain Captain Hume; and two parties of one hundred men and seventy men each acted as supports, one on either flank of the main body.

The naval brigade from the men-of-war in harbour furnished the reserve, which took post in the spur in front of Peterborough tower.

---

85. *Second Journal.*

86. *London Gazette; Exact Journal; Second Journal.*

87. *London Gazette; Exact Journal.*

88. *London Gazette.*

89. *Exact Journal.* Thacker.

90. A letter from Tangier Bay, 17 May, 1680; *Exact Journal;* Thacker.

91. Captain Hume, as well as Hacket and Hodge of the same regiment and probably also of the Grenadier company, has had his name handed down to posterity in a doggrel drinking song of the regiment which may be given here at the end of the chapter, as a specimen of the military poetical taste of the period.

92. *Exact journal. London Gazette.*

Lieutenant Spragg in command.

Between Charles Fort and the town lay three deep trenches.[93] The most formidable was that nearest the town, and this was twelve or fourteen feet in depth and twenty in width. A good deal of rain had fallen lately [94] and the ditches were rendered worse by the quantity of mud and water at the bottom.

Unfortunately, the garrison of Charles Fort acquainted Henrietta Fort through a speaking-trumpet of the intended evacuation. Now the Moors had been in possession of Henrietta for a day or two, but had craftily retained everything in such a state (and without removing the garrison), as to keep the surrender a secret from the town and from Charles Fort. Although, for better security, all communications were made in Irish at this time, yet the Moors managed to discover the purport of this one, and made ready to take advantage of their knowledge.

At about half-past seven o'clock Captain St John led the men out of Charles Fort,[95] with his grenadiers to the front. Captain Trelawney brought up the rear. Beside him trotted his little son,[94] "*haud passibus equis.*" Ensign Roberts remained behind to blow up the guns and material.[96] The men advanced boldly and in good order to the first trench. It was full of Moors. After a short sharp struggle the enemy was beaten out, and the trench crossed. At the same moment Roberts fired his train.

At the second ditch great slaughter was made of the Moors, who stood thicker than before: they were forced back, and the party had now the worst part of their task before them. On pressed the grenadiers, briskly using their firelocks. Close followed the musketeers and pikemen. On every side pressed a crowd of turbaned enemies; in every direction the brilliant sunshine gleamed on hostile weapons, spears, scimitars, and daggers, while the way was obscured by the smoke of innumerable matchlocks and pistols. The press of the swarming enemy was at times so great that the imprisoned Englishmen seemed to make no progress at all. The men were dropping fast. But the third trench is quite close now, and on the other side can be distinguished the red coats and white facings of Hume's Grenadiers.

---

93. *London Gazette.* Letter from Tangier. Plans. Thacker.
94. Letter from Tangier.
95. *London Gazette.* Thacker. For a full account of this day's affairs see also *Letter from Tangier,* 18 May, 1680, Dartmouth MSS.
96. *London Gazette.*

Captain Hume and his party of the Royals were not standing idle all this time. Through the gaps in the English lines which the enemy had cut, rode the Moorish cavalry, but Hume was ready for them. Then, as now, British infantry feared no cavalry in the world. With the pikemen forming the outside of the square, and the musqueteers firing over their protruded pikes, the men of the Royals stood charge after charge [97] with the courage and steadiness for which they had long been famous.

Their work was, however, child's play compared with the terrible agony that had fallen to the lot of their brethren of the Second. Close nearing the last trench, on came St John, Trelawney and their "lambs." The Moors, furious at seeing their prey escaping them, raged wildly round. The little band was already much reduced in number, but still on they pressed. To be captured was eternal slavery; to lie down wounded was to await a death of barbarous torture. Liberty and home, and all that was dear to the breast of each one, lay on the other side of that black trench.

A spurt for dear life, a thickening of the swarthy savage mob around, a desperate effort, and the ditch lies just in front. The tired men see that it is deeper than the others, and with slush enough in it to smother any wounded wretch that should fall. However it must be crossed. Captain St. John, cheering them on, made a rush and managed to get safely over.[98] Facing about at once, he assisted his men, notwithstanding a wound in the shoulder. The Moors, chagrined and half mad with rage, crowd on to the English.

The soldiers in the rear, over-anxious to cross the ditch, forget to maintain their order, and, hindered by their own men in front, they are slaughtered easily by the infuriated Moors. Young Roberts who had overtaken the party got over safely,[98] so did Lieutenant Clause and thirty-nine men. Poor Trelawney [99] reached the last ditch with his men, but stopping to help his little boy down he was killed.[100] The child was captured, as were fourteen of the soldiers.[100] The deep trench was turned into a huge grave, for of the one hundred and eighty persons that had marched out of Charles Fort an hour before, more than one hundred and twenty were now headless corpses. The barbarous Moors vented their disappointed rage on those who in life

97. *London Gazette*. Thacker. *Letter from Tangier*, Dartmouth MSS.
98. *London Gazette*.
99. Letter from Tangier.
100. *London Gazette. Letter from Tangier.*

had defied them, by mutilating their dead bodies. Of Hume's company fifteen were killed, and Captain Hume himself with three other officers and many of the men were wounded. Hume received his wound as the party retired on the supports covering the small remainder of the unfortunate garrison of Charles Fort. Alcaid Garbuz,[101] one of the most distinguished of the enemy's generals, led a last charge on the retreating Englishmen.

Making straight at Hume he rode over him and struck at him, but he struck his last blow, for his horse stumbled over his prostrate foe, the Moor came heavily to the ground and one of Hume's men dashed his brains out as he fell.

While this action was taking place, as well to seize the opportunity to evacuate another fort, as to create a diversion in favour of Charles Fort, an attempt was being made to get off thirteen men from Giles Fort; Giles Fort was a small redoubt on the beach close to Whitby. Admiral Herbert lay off with his ship, and the boats of the fleet were sent in to fire on the Moors and favour the escape of the party from the redoubt. The boats lay as near as they could without running the risk of being boarded by the enemy.

The Moors were as thick as bees, and surrounded the fort thirsting for the blood of its occupants with all the savage cruelty distinctive of their race and their religion. Had the boats touched the beach they would have swarmed over them in an instant The sailors shouted to the soldiers to make a dash for it. The Moors were firing so thickly that it appeared certain death to leave the shelter of the redoubt. The water was deep, and the soldiers feared to be drowned if they escaped the shot. The sailors were being picked off, and a Mr. Wray, a young gentleman volunteer in the *Adventure's* boat was killed. In vain the officers urged the soldiers on the shore to hasten. Only one man had the nerve to face the double danger of shot and deep waters. He escaped; the remaining twelve surrendered to the Moors.

Although the garrison had suffered a severe loss of men in this action, and although the enemy had now all the outposts in their power, the moral effect of the bravery displayed by the English troops was yet so great that five days later Omar Ben Haddn sent in an offer for a four months' truce. His conditions were that the garrison should withdraw themselves within the limits formerly occupied by the Portuguese. Several reasons combined to induce the governor to accede to the terms proposed.

101. *Second Journal. London Gazette.*

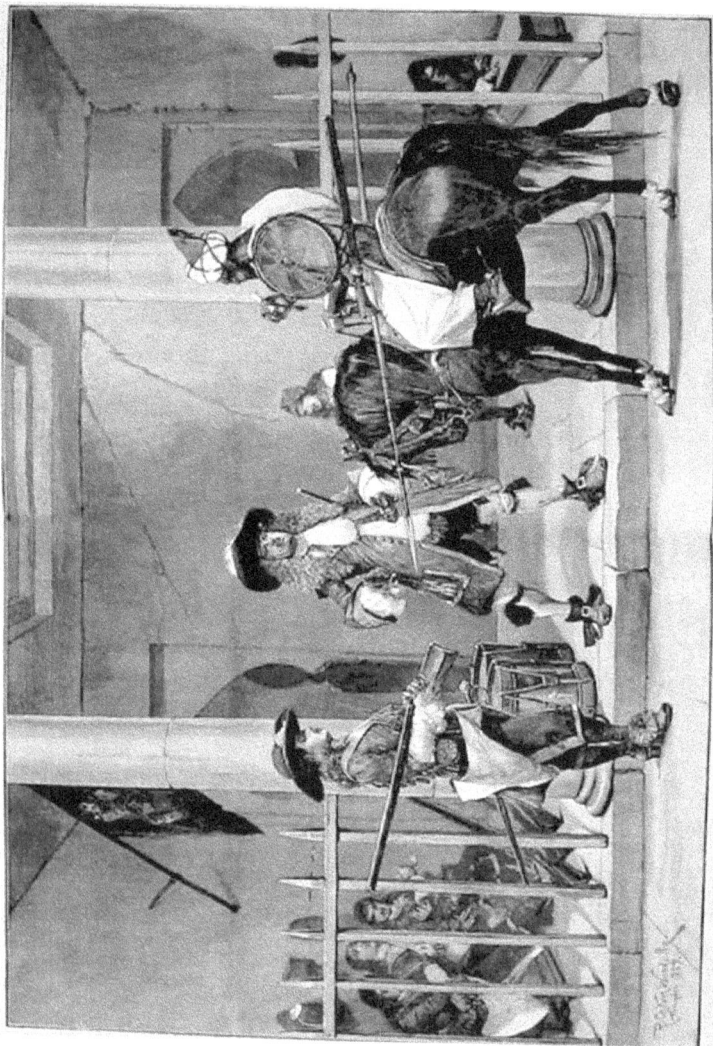

TANGIER UNDER THE ENGLISH

The Moors had now complete possession of a large part of the English lines: working from the forts they had lately acquired, nothing could prevent them from ultimately cutting off all the other forts in like manner: they had gained a vast advantage for their future operations by the capture of the guns in Charles and Henrietta Forts: any delay must be of advantage to the garrison, for a considerable reinforcement had been promised from home: the Moors had so improved in their engineering, their gunnery,[102] and their discipline, that without a large addition to the strength of the garrison there was grave reason to fear an attempt to take the town by storm, when their numbers would afford them a fair possibility of success; lastly, it would be of greater advantage to the English than to the Moors to obtain a rest through the hot season.

The truce being arranged, mutual visits of courtesy were made. The English were astonished to see how indefatigably their enemy had availed himself of every chance. It was known that the Moors had obtained a number of guns by their late successes, but it was wondered whence they would obtain cannon balls. But now a huge supply was exhibited to the English visitors to the Moorish camp. Omar had always anticipated the acquisition of artillery, and with commendable foresight he had for years past collected the cannon balls[33] fired from the garrison.

The interval of the truce was occupied by the English in repairing damages to the lines, and in bringing guns from the Straits side and mounting them on the land side of the town. Urgent solicitations for reinforcements were sent to England. Lord Inchiquin,[103] whom Sir Palmes Fairborne came out to relieve, went home in June, and personally urged upon the authorities the necessity for complying with the demand for aid.

A regiment of Foot was raised and was known as the Second Tangier Regiment.[104] It was, however, not dispatched to Tangier in time to take a share in the fighting. It has since made itself a name as the Fourth Regiment of Foot.

During the period of the truce large reinforcements were dispatched from England, and on its expiration embassies, messages, and

102. *Second Journal.*
103. *London Gazette.*
104. Order for raising the Regt., 13 July, 1680; W. O. records; and Home Office records. Abstract of Forces 1680, Brit. Mus., Add. MSS. 10,123. After return from Tangier in 1684, it received the title of The Duchess of York and Albany's Regt.; List of the Officers, &c., May, 1684, Home Office records. Nathan Brooks, &c.

illuminated letters [105] took the place of hostilities. However, no long time had elapsed before the English reverted to their old trick of annexing plots of territory,[106] and the war would probably have shortly broken out again had not the English government decided on abandoning Tangier altogether.[107] The troops thereupon returned home in 1684.[108]

105. Thacker; *London Gazette*, &c. Guy in his Secret Service payments for June quarter, 1682. "To Gideon Roger for writing, flourishing and embellishing partly in gold, a letter sent to the Emperor of Fez and Morocco by (hands of) Colonel Kirke, £10." Among the reinforcements was a troop under Major Oglethorpe, formed of 80 Gentlemen from the three troops of Guards, and one troop of the Blues; R. War-rts., 2 June and 7 June, 1680, W. O. records.
106. Thacker.
107. Abstract of Forces 1680, Brit. Mus., Add. MSS. 10,123, in this abstract the forces paid as pertaining to the garrison of Tangier are Coy's, Langston's, Neatby's and Mackenzie's troops of Horse.

			Privates.
These were reduced into Dragoons when "they came to England"	4 troops	=	160
Royal Regt. of Foot (1st Foot)	21 compies.	=	1,050
Tangier Regt. (2nd Foot)	12 ,,	=	600
Trelawny's (4th Foot)	16 ,,	=	1,200
			3,010

This regiment was raised 14 July, 1680, and sent to Tangier; and when returned to England in 1684, 5 Companies were sent to Ireland and 11 remained here." In Nathan Brooks's *List*, 1684, this regt. is styled "The Duchess of York and Albany's Regt. of Foot"; in the Est. List, 1685, Add. MSS. 15,897, Brit Mus., and in Chamberlayne, 1687, "Queen's Regt. of Foot," the Second Foot being then styled the "Queen Dowager's."
108. In the 1st vol. of Colonel Davis's *Hist of the 2nd Queen's Regt.*, Lond. 1887, will be found an exhaustive account of the British occupation of Tangier, replete with curious details.

"A Proper New Ballad, Entitled 'The Granadeers Rant'"

1). Captain Hume is bound to sea.
Hey boys, ho boys;
Captain Hume is bound to sea,
Ho:
Captain Hume is bound to sea,
And his brave companie;
Hey the brave Granadeers,
Ho.

2). We'll drink no more Irish beer.
Hey boys, ho boys;
We'll drink no more Irish beer
Ho:
We'll drink no more Irish beer.
For we're all bound to Tangeer
Hey the brave Grenadiers,
Ho.

3). We'll drink the Spanish wine,
Hey boys, ho boys;
We'll drink the Spanish wine
Ho:
We'll drink the Spanish wine.
And court their ladies fine.
Hey the brave Grenadiers,
Ho.

4). Now we're upon the Sound,
Hey boys, ho boys;
Now we're upon the Sound

Ho:
Now we're upon the Sound,
Every man's health goes round,
Hey the brave Grenadiers,
Ho.

5).When we came to C . . . . on shore,
Hey boys, ho boys;
When we came to C . . . . on shore
Ho:
When we came to C . . . . on shore.
We made the guns to roar.
Hey the brave Grenadiers,
Ho.

6).Now we drink the Spanish wine,
Hey boys, ho boys;
Now we drink the Spanish wine, ,
Ho:
Now we drink the Spanish wine.
And kiss their ladies fine.
Hey the brave Scottish boys,
Ho.

7).When we do view Tangier,
Hey boys, ho boys;
When we do view Tangier
Ho:
When we do view Tangier,
We'll make these proud Moors to fear,
Hey the brave Grenadiers,
Ho.

8).When we came to Tangier shore.
Hey boys, ho boys;
When we came to Tangier shore.
Ho:
When we came to Tangier shore,
We'll make our granadoes roar.
Hey the brave Grenadiers,
Ho.

9).When we come upon the Mould,
Hey boys, ho boys;

When we come upon the Mould,
Ho:
When we come upon the Mould,
We'll make these proud Moors to yield,
Hey the brave Scottish boys.
Ho.

10). When we come upon the wall.
Hey boys, ho boys;
When we come upon the wall,
Ho:
When we come upon the wall,
We'll make these proud Moors to fall.
Hey the brave Grenadiers,
Ho.

11). There's Hacket, Hume, and Hodge,
Hey boys, ho boys;
There's Hacket, Hume, and Hodge,
Ho:
There's Hacket, Hume, and Hodge,
In Charles's Fort shall lodge,
Hey the brave Grenadiers,
Ho.

12). Hacket led on the Van,
Hey boys, ho boys;
Hacket led on the Van,
Ho;
Hacket led on the Van,
Where was killed many a man.
Hey the brave Scottish boys,
Ho.

13). Sixty brave Grenadiers,
Hey boys, ho boys;
Sixty brave Grenadiers,
Ho:
Sixty brave Grenadiers,
Beat the Moors from Tangiers,
Hey the brave Scottish boys,
Ho.

The Diary of Sir James Halkett: Tangier—1680

(Readers should note the diary is reproduced in the language and spelling of the day and original documents).

INTRODUCTION

It is the *Diary* kept by Sir James Halkett, Major in Dumbarton's Regiment, now "The Royal Scots (The Royal Regiment)," in the year 1680, at Tangier, and must be one of the earliest specimens of a War Diary.

The narrative ends abruptly and seems never to have been completed by Sir James, probably owing to his death in October, 1684, shortly after his return to England.

Tangier had been in possession of the English since 1661, and Halkett had served there when the Earl of Teviot was Governor, 1663-4. In 1680, in response to urgent appeals from the governor for reinforcements, 4 companies of Dumbarton's Regiment were dispatched from Ireland in H.M. ships *James, Swan*, and *Garland*, arriving at Tangier on 4 April, in time for the severe engagements with the Moors in April and May. These were followed by 12 more Companies in H.M. ships *Ruby, Phoenix, Garland*, and *Guernsey*, which arrived on 30 July, under the command of "the valorous Hackett, Major to that renowned regiment of the Earl of Dunbarton" (Ross), who further describes the men of Dumbarton's as:

> Of approved valour, whose fame echoed the sound of the glorious actions and achievements in France and other nations, leaving behind them a report of their glorious victories wherever they came both at home and abroad; every place witnessing and giving large testimony to their renown.

The logs of the *Ruby* and *Phoenix* are now in the Public Record Office, London, and give interesting details of the companies and their experiences during the voyage.

Four independent companies, from Ireland, were added to Dumbarton's 16, and the whole were temporarily formed into a regiment in two battalions, under Halkett, and ordered to take precedence as Dumbarton's, "that is to say, next after the Guards." These companies of Dumbarton's took part in all the subsequent fighting, remaining in garrison at Tangier till 1684, when the place was abandoned.

Halkett, and other officers in the regiment are mentioned in "*A proper new Ballad, entitled 'The Granadeers Rant,'*" published in 1681, one verse of which is here given:—

> *There's Hacket, Hume and Hodge,*
> *Hey boyes, ho boyes;*
> *There's Hacket, Hume and Hodge, ho!*
> *There's Hacket, Hume and Hodge,*
> *In Charles's Fort shall lodge,*
> *Hey the brave Granadeers, ho!*

A series of pictures by Stoop at Patshull, in possession of Lord Dartmouth, depict several episodes of the period at Tangier. In one, the interesting figures of four pipers, evidently of Dumbarton's, are to be seen playing on the Mole during its destruction, prior to the embarkation for home.

Dumbarton's embarked in H.M. ships *Henrietta, Oxford, Foresight, Dragon,* and *Grafton*. Again interesting details of the voyage can be gleaned from the logs. The captain of the *Henrietta* notes how, on meeting a French man-of-war. he "fired two shot to make her strike sails."

Halkett's *Diary* is of great regimental interest to The Royal Scots, being a detailed account by one of its earliest commanding officers, of the regiment's first active service abroad, since its final return to England from France in 1678. In the words of the Regimental Records "Dumbarton's came to Tangier with a great reputation, and when they left it, that reputation was greatly enhanced."

Halkett had served twelve years (1668-80) in Dumbarton's. In 1679 he was with his company at Bandon. In 1684 he was at Rochester and on 1 May was promoted to be Lieut.-Colonel and commanded Dumbarton's at the Review on Putney Heath on 1 October (Nathan Brooks), in which month he died, being succeeded in command by

Sir Archibald Douglas.

C. Dalton (*The Scots Army*. 1061—1688. 1909.) states that Halkett was one of the Halketts of Pitfirrane, but the court of the Lord Lyon is unable to confirm this, or to trace Sir James in any way. Nor is it clear when or by whom he was knighted.

THE DIARY.

A short and true account of the most remarkable things that passed during the late wars with the Moors at Tangier in the year 1680, and Treaty of Peace betwixt the Alcad Domar & Lt. Collonel Sackville. By Sr. James Halket comander of 16 Companies and Major of the E. of Dunbarton's Regiment there. Copied from a MSS. written with his own hand.

There has been so many different relations of the transactions at Tangier from the time of looseing of Charles Fort till the time that the King of Moroco sent his embassadour to England, what be lyes and partialities and mistakes that it is hard for the king to find out the truth, I designe here to give a short and true account of the most remarkable things that passed during the late wars with the Moors in the year 1680 and treatie of peace betwixt the Alcad Domar and Lieutenant Collonel Sackville.[1]

I having had the honour to command 16 Companies of the Earle of Dumbarton's Regiment during that war there in the station of major; and, having served there under an able Master the Earl of Tiviot[2] at the time of his war there, who was a man of an extraordinary genie beside his long service and experience in the wars who shewed his admirable conduct in the taking in and fortifying of that ground about Tangier with redouts and lines in so short a time with so small

---

1. Captain in the Guards. Was appointed on 31 May, 1680, to be Lieut.-Colonel of a Regiment of Foot, called "The King's Battalion," composed of 2 Companies from the 1st Regiment of Guards and 1 Company each from the Coldstream Guards, the Duke of York's Regiment (the "Maritime" Regiment, disbanded in 1689), and the Earl of Musgrave's Regiment (now The Buffs), then formed for service at Tangier. On the death of Sir P. Fairborne, Sackville became Governor, and C.-in-C. at Tangier. He was promoted to the rank of Colonel in 1685; and to that of Major-General in 1688. He retired from the service in 1688.

2 Andrew Rutherford. Created Lord Rutherford 1661 and appointed Governor of Dunkirk, 1662. Created Earl of Teviot and appointed Governor of Tangier, 1663. Killed in action at Tangier, May, 1664. Had been a lieut.-general in the French service, and commanded Rutherford's Regiment, 1643, which was incorporated in Dumbarton's in 1660. See *The Scots Peerage*, VII., and 'D.N.B.'

a garrison as he had under his command in spite of all the force that Galland[3] could bring against him to oppose his proceedings which was greater than any that has been before Tangier since his time.

I having besides since that time served in France in Dumbarton's Regiment the space of 12 years in countreys where the war was most active, in the station of captain and major where certainly the (. . . . .)[4] of the war is at the greatest perfection which makes me presume to think that I am as capable to make observations and to give a good account of the proceedings in the late war in Tangier which may be readable, in some manner to the king in his concerns there and that he may know who served His Majesty there.

So soon as I got my orders at Dubline to cause our 12 companies that was ordered with me for Tangier to move from their several garrisons to Cork where we was all to assemble and immediately after being ordered with all the diligence imaginable upon my peril to ship the said companies a board the king's frigate that was lying ready waiting for us in the harbour of Kinsail to receive us, which was taske hard enoughe for one officer to make soldiers march the king's service in Tangier, requireing such haste in order to so great a weight that we could not expect to have the time gett what arrears was due to us, there being a 12 months arrears due to out soldiers; upon my receiving my orders at Dubline I did solicite my Lord D. of Or[5] to have power to take what men that was good of those 5 companies of ours that did remaine in Ireland—which his Gr. gave me his order for the doing it for the making up compleat the 12 ordered for Tangier.

And his grace was sensible that I had sufficiently managed my business with care and dilligence in everything that was requisite for one officer to doe to hinder desertion of our soldiers till our shipping; on the day after all our companies that was ordered was assembled at Cork I got the news from Mr. St. Elies of that cessation of arms for six months that was agreed on immediately after the lossing of Charles Fort and the rest of the redouts about the time which not only gave us time to receive our arrears that was due to us but likeways 3 moneths pay of advance for all the 20 companies that was commanded from Ireland to Tangier which I carried over with me which was a very great encouragement to us besides the news that came immediately

---

3. Ab'd Allah Ghailan, *i.e.,* Gayland, Guyland, etc. (Roiith).
4. Blank in the original. ? science.
5. Duke of Ormonde, Lord-Lieutenant of Ireland.
6. Thomas Butler, Earl of Ossory, eldest son of James, (continued next page),

after that the king had made choice of my Lord Osserie [6] to go command in that expedition which was extreamly agreeable to us to serve under his command.

I shipt our 12 companies the day and sailed the next day and I landed at Tangier August, I was the first that brought the news of my Lo. Osserie's coming to be a general which was very agreeable to everyone.

Upon the orders Sir Pames[7] had from court to cause Mr. Bekman[8] the ingenier make a designe and draught of a fortification that he judged most necessare and convenient for the situation of Tangier and the fortification of those sand hills east from the town towards old Tangier where the Moores can conveniently make their batteries to annoy the ships in the harbour, after the ingenier had finished his designe of fortification to be sent to the king and had computed as near as could the charge and expenies that the work would cost which was great and vast, Sir.Pames assembled August the field officers, Admiral Herbert[9] Mr. Shers[10] in council to give their opinions whether they approved of that designe to be sent to the king or thought it absolutely necessare where everie one did agree for the designe of the harbour, that it was and certainly it were so if you look upon the Moores to be formidable as to be able to maintaine ane army before Tangier with canon and amunition, which I believe they are not able to doe for many good reasons, we continued with the expectation of the arrival of my Lord of Osserie with a considerable body of horse and foot till we got the news of his sickness and soon after his death.

During the rest of the time of the Cessation of Arms, Sr. Pames was much imployed in causing make conveniences for the troops he expected from England and the troops in exercising but I believe the great expence and charge of that designe of fortification with the misfortunate death of my Lord Osserie made the king resolve to endeavour to have peace upon reasonable terms without fortifying, upon

1st Duke of Ormonde. Appointed Governor of Tangier, but died in London in July, 1680, before taking up the appointment. See 'D.N.B.'
7. Sir Palmes Fairborne, who had served at Tangier for 18 years. See 'D.N.B.'
8. Martin Beckman. See 'D.N.B.'
9. Captain (local Vice-Admiral) Arthur Herbert, R.N. Appointed to command the Station, July, 1680. Created Earl of Torrington, 1689. See 'D.N.B.'
10. Henry Sheeres. Engineer in chief at Tangier (1669-83); built many of the forts and the Mole. See 'D.N.B.' and *Proceedings of the R.A. Institution*. Vol. xix. Some MSS. notes entitled "Journal of Proceedings," dated September-October, 1680, by Sheeres. exist in the Public Record Office, .CO. 279/26.

with instructions from court Sir Pames sent out the Moorish merchant to the Alcad Domar to offer to enter into terms with him for a settled peace the *alcad* answered that he remembered that in Gailand's time when Tiviot was governour in his absence in England the lieutenant governour judgeing that the time of the cessation would expire before the governour returned, did agree with Gailand to prolong the cessation for six months longer,.

The governour arriveing soon after and finding this done was extreamely displeased with the lieut, governour being he had no instructions for it and he haveing orders from the king to go immediately about the secureing of as much ground as he judged necessarie for the use of the Garrison would not stand to that agreement of the lieut, go. with Gailand, did immediately begin his working, so he knew that Sir Pames was but lieutenant governour and that he was informed that there was a governour coming over, so he would not treat with him fearing to be served in the same manner, the time of the cessation of arms being short. Sir Pames assembled a council of war August of the field officers and all the captains to have their opinion whether they thought it convenient or fitting to undertake anything without the town immediately after the expireing of the cessation or to wait for the horse from England or the horse that was promised from Spain after that several had reasoned upon the business and gave their opinions *pro* and *con.*, Lieut.-Collonel Sakvil's opinion was that it would be a foolish and dangerous thing to undertake anything without the Town without horse against ane enemy that he believes was mighty and powerful without especially expecting horse and foot from England and knowing the many misfortunes that had alreadie befallen that garrison with rash undertakings.

My opinion was that it was fitting to undertake some thing with out the town so soon as peace expired without waiting more force considering what a powerful garrison was already in Tangier consisting of about 3,000 foot and a troop of 30 horse so well composed of so many good officers and soldiers which the like was never in Tangier and certainly it could not but plainly and clearly appear to any man of sense that had seen anything of war that there could have been done several things with out town, as the making of some places of arms before Katrina Gate and so gone on gradually which certainly could have been done without exposeing the foot to any danger or the fearing considerable loss for the Moores could not nor durst not undertake the hindering us let their number have been what it will so near the town for there was no need of horse in the beginning and it was very uncertain when those troops that was expected from England should come or whether they would come at all, the resolutions did so change in England concerning Tangier,.

Now if there had comed none and if he had waited for them it would have made those that knew not the Moores believe them to be so mighty a people that nothing could be undertaken against them without a considerable army: in the contrair if we went out and made those places of arms which certainly can be done without risk it would be a great encouragement to what troops came afterwards. After all the reasonings it was put to the vote whether we should go out, it was carried be the major votes that we should go out, notwithstanding Sir Pames resolved to undertake nothing without, till he got more horse,.

The next day Admial Herbert sailed with the fleet that was before Tangier to Gibraltar to bring over those Spanish horse that was promised, when he came there was no news, of those Spanish horse: the admiral returned immediately to Tangier again, but those ships with the 3 troops of English horse appeared from England which came in good time and was landed as soon as possible could, their horse in a pretty good condition after so long a voyage; the time of peace being within a few days of expireing Sir Pames, finding that it was not clear what day the peace ended, being their reckoning and ours differed, sent out to know of the *alcad* the day; the *alcad* answered he would let him know when it did, within two days the *alcad* sent Hamett[11] the Moore that had served in England in the duke's troop and told that the time of the peace was out and that the nixt day he would to wars.

Admiral Herbert landed about 500 of the seamen, he having orders to attend with the fleet during the war, composed of so many companies with a company of grenadiers, with the compleat number of officers to each company, of the sea-officer, and volunteers he made choice of Captain George Barthell who formerly had been a captain in my Lord Dumbarton's Regiment, to command that battalion of seamen in quality of major under him; the 3 troops of English horse newly landed had several days after the expireing of the peace to refresh their horses and in exerciseing in order for the design of action without, after Sir Pames had disposed everything in the best order for

11. Hamet, a renegade Moor, who had been sent to Europe and educated, but who, on his return, deserted and placed his knowledge and skill at the service of the *alcade*. (Routh.)

the designe of working without, in causing what pallisads and instruments for working the ingenier judged necessar for that design of work without to the spur without Katrina Gate .

The night before we went out Sir Pames sent for me to the castle where I found him in his closet after talking of the design of the work he intended next day to begin without, and of the number of troops he intended to sustain that work with, he desired me to tell him what way I judged to the best advantage to dispose the troops in battle for the sustaining the workmen: after I gave him my opinion to the best of my understanding, he told he thought my way was well, but not altogether in form, for he designed the troops all in one line, with the 4 troops of horse upon the wings, for he said there was some critick that censured him in all things, meaning Sakvill and Talmach[12] they believing to understand more of form than he. I told him everyone that commanded did dispose their troops in battle to the best advantage according to the situation of the field of battle they were on, and to the designe they had in hand. After he had taken my advice in several things I left him and went about the disposing things for the next days work.

It being the 18th of September we marched out with the whole force of the garrison, leaving only the ordinar guards within, the 4 troops of horse first then the detachment of 300 men designed to be our advanced men commanded by Lieut. Collonell Talmash, that honour was put upon him I believe upon the account of his quality and being a man of interest at court in prejudice of Captain Bowes[13] that was the older captain, and his tour the troops was imbattelled as it was designed all in one line: our right hand being covered he the old line of communication betwixt the town and Polfort,[14] and our left be (Nord[15] Redout) which was still in being then, the discoveries[16] being made as far out as was judged necessare, and [. . . .][17] in the most fitting places, some little fireing being made at our discoveries be some few scattring Moores, not yet any body of men appearing nor any guard upon that hand.

---

12. Captain Thomas Tollemache, who commanded the Coldstream Company in the "King's Battalion," under Sackville. Subsequently a Lieut.-General, and Colonel of the 5th Foot, See 'D.N.B.'
13. George B. of the 1st Regiment of Foot Guards, now commanding a Company in the "King's Battalion," at Tangier.
14. Pole Fort.
15. "Nord Redoubt" has been inserted in the original MSS. It should be Norwood, so called after Colonel Henry Norwood, who had served at Tangier earlier.
16. Reconnaissances.
17. Blank in original.

Then Lieut. Collonel Talmash with his 300 men was commanded to post himself about the mines of Polfort, then an ingeneer went about the viewing of the ground about Polfort after he resolved upon the design of the work, it was resolved to cause word[18] a battalion at time so many hours: the battalion of seamen being posted on the east of the town, the rest standing to their arms and it being necessare to advance fire men[19] upon all hands of Polfort to keep the enemy off and in skirmish in favour of our workmen; the detachments being made was posted at three several places some shelter being made in haste for the men, the Moores about this time appeared with several colloures from the bottom near Mes River[20] where they camped, I judge about the number of 600 or 700 men all foot very few horse [. . . .][21] that they came very scatteredly fearing our cannon and posted themselves at the ruines of James Fort and at Anne Fort and upon the auld lane betwixt the two forts: the advanced men that keeped our advanced posts in skirmish all the day over, where we had some few men killed and wounded.

I am very confident at this time the Moores could not make a 1,000 men before the town: we continued all that day till 7 a clock at night in working about Polfort and in relieving our workmen and the advanced posts from time to time till that pallisad about the ruins—of the fort was done, and a breastwork within the pallisad, and the place put as the best posture of defence. For the night following Lieut. Coll. Sak. with the battalion of guards took possession of the place to make guard that night there being a detachment of 300 men of reserve left in the place of arms before Katrina gate; we then retired our advanced and work men and marched into town, we having that day's work much easier than we imagined.

The next day we marched out the same number of men and keeped the same method we did the day before, things passed much about the same manner it did the day before; I relieved Lieut. Coll. Sakvile with our first battalion and 200 men of our second, then the troops retired to town, the 3rd day we marched out as we did before

18. ? work.
19. Musketeers, as distinct from pikemen.
20. Mes River has been inserted in the original: it is meant for Jews River.
21. Blank in original.
22. Blank in original.
23. Robert Hodges. Captain-Lieutenant in Sir John Talbot's Dragoons, 5 October, 1678 ("Dalton"). Captain in Dumbarton's in April, 1679. ("Omonde" papers). Served at Tangier, as Captain of the Grenadier Company. (Continued next page).

after the [. . .][22] and our advanced men posted, Capt. Hoges[23] our captain. Our company of granadeers, desired Sir Pames liberty to go to our advanced post upon the line betwixt Monmouth and James Fort with his company of granadeers to skirmish, Sir Pames after his earnest intreatie condescended to it, having recommended it to him not to engage himself further than the advanced post. Hoges told me of thing, marched with his company his drums beatting,[24] the Moores seeing this expected something extraordihar, put them all to their arms about the town and drew them all to that hand; Hoges having advanced about a 100 yards before our advanced post to a little trench that the enemy possest, and having beat them out that was there, and taken possession of the trench, the Moores upon all hands drew together about James Fort, advanced with about five or six hundred men where they entered into skirmish with Hoges, he finding it too hote for him, being no equality of number, was forced to retire somewhat precipitantly to our advanced post again, with the loss of three men and of his company and several wounded.

I being with Sir Pames at that time about some other concerns and hearing the skirmish was hote at that post, I galloped to the post, our company of granadeers being retireing at that same time and the Moores following after, which astonished our men posted there a little, so that they were reeling, I having sent to cause advance Capt. Lauriston with his troop of horse that was near, a purpose to sustain our advanced men, which gave again assurance to our foot, so that they continued the skirmish hotely for some time, where we had several men killed and wounded, the Moores being more exposed to our fire than we to their thought it convenient to retire, but advanced with collours all round nearer an advanced post, which made the skirmishing hoter than formerly all the rest of the day at those posts; when the time drew near that we usually retired to town, I told Sir Pames that I believed that they designed to undertake something against us upon our retiring our advanced post, they having continued strong about James Fort since the skirmish.

In the morning, he told me he had the same thoughts, I said that

Eventually Lieut. Colonel, and then Colonel of Colonel Archibald Douglas's Regiment (16th) of Foot, at the head of which he was killed at Steenkirk, 1692. Ross, in his *Tangers Rescue*, gives a personal description of Captain Hodges' valour and activity. 24. No doubt the well-known tune of "Dumbarton's Drums," played to this day by The Royal Scots; also known as "The Scots March," and well-known on the battlefields of Europe during the 30 Years' War. Heard by Pepys at Rochester in 1667 and noted by him as still being played in 1680. (Records of *The Royal Scots*.)

there was at the advanced post and on the line betwixt the post and Monmouth fort above 300 men, what of ours and other detachments, that was made to sustain our advanced post, and that our captain that commanded our advance was a young man that never before had seen action, Captain Forbes,[25] and prayed him to give me leave to undertake the management of the retreat, he was pleased I made the offer, and ordered me to go about the doing it and to take what men of ours I judged necessare for the doing it, there was 200 firemen of our second battalion, commanded be Captain Londie[26] and Captain Moncriefe,[27] that had been on the guard with me the night before at Polfort, that had continued within the pallisads all the day without skirmishing or working.

I made choice of them for the business and marched them up to a convenient place near Monmouth Fort, where they could not be seen be the enemy, and ordered them to continue there in readyness, without showing themselves, till the rear of our advanced men came their length, and if the Moores followed, I would be with them in time to do with them as I judged convenient: I then went up to our advanced post I caused retire some rest of amunition that was there, I then endeavoured to make our men retire a file or two at a time so that the Moores might not perceive, but they very well observed our motions, perceived we intended to retire, they advanced with their collours from the mines of James Fort and from all the places on that hand.

I put our best men on our rear and retired homewards, the Moores was very soon with us on our rear, I judge the number of 500 men within and without that old line that runes from James Fort to Monmouth fort, then they began to bestow their fire amongst us and keeped close on our reer till we came the length of our 200 men commanded be Captains Londie and Moncrieff, so soon as our rear

25. Francis Forbes, a young captain in Dumbarton's, who died of wounds received in action on 24 October, 1680.
26. Robert Lundy, a Captain in Dumbarton's in April, 1679. ("Ormonde" Papers). Wounded 27.10.1680. Lieut.-Colonel of Colonel Mountjoy's Regiment in Ireland. Colonel of a Regiment of Foot in Ireland which was never formed. Governor of Londonderry. Adjutant-General to the Portuguese Army. Taken prisoner in Spain and exchanged. (*Dalton*).
27. James Moncrieff. Youngest son of Sir John Moncrieff, Bart., whom he succeeded as 4th Bart. Captain in Dumbarton's in April, 1679. ("Ormonde" papers). Wounded 14 May, 1680. Served at Sedgemoor, wounded. Awarded gratuity of £40. Lieut.-Colonel of Sir Wm. Beveridge's Regiment (16th Foot), 1690. Colonel, as Sir James, of a newly-raised regiment in Scotland, afterwards known as Colonel George Hamilton's Regiment, 1693. (Dalton).

past them, I run and caused them advance and made a fresh discharge on those Moores that was on the inside of the line, they not expecting to find fresh men so near them, they passed all of them very precipitantly to the outside of the line.

I made our men to the right hand about, and marched down the hill till we was quite out of sight of the enemy; upon this all the Moores believed we was running, came precipitantly after us our men having be that time charged[28] again, I made our men face about again, being very near one and other, where we continued in skirmish a long half hour against all that had followed us, we having some advantage of the ground be some old lines and places that gave us some covert against their fire, we having them still exposed with full bodie to our fire, where certainly we killed many of their men, the Moores having spent their amunition, they continued for some time in throwing of great stones amongst us, but they finding our fire too sharp for them, they found it convenient to retire, so we ended that days work very well and retired in town with the troops.

The night after, and the next day there fell a great deall of rain, so we did not move out a town but made some detachments for the working within that pallisad about the new work, and all the carpenters being imployed in makeing up of Paul's Fort to cover the men within from that time to the [. . . .][29] we continued without moveing out of town, but with the relief to Polfort every day, and the detachments for working after the fort was put into some posture of defence, and having raised a battrie for three pieces of cannon within, and a work that was cannon proofe ther, we began a new line of communication straight from Katrina Gate to the fort, the report having past in the countrey of our being master of that place again, and they expecting that we should a proceeded in undertaking more, brought all the force, I judge they could well send or maintain, against us.

The weather then growing unconstant, which hindered us to move out as we did the first 3 dayes, the Moores who made better use of their time and finding us grow a little slack in our business, they took possession of that ground about Monmouth Fort where they made a fashion of places of arms and carryed on a trench from that to the old place, made by Tiviot about a 200 yards before the fort, and round all upon the right hand of the fort which was a good as a line of countervalation to them.

---

28. Having charged their musquets again; *i.e.,* reloaded.
29. Blank in original.

61

Sir Pames upon the instructions he had to endeavour to have peace upon reasonable terms, it was resolved in council of war that the governour should make an offer to enter into a treatie of peace with them, and to assure them there was no other governour to come to Tangier, and that he had full power to make a peace with them, for as long time as he thought fit, which they accepted, Sir Pames made choice of Lieut. Coll. Tollmach to go to them with his instructions, and the articles proposed, so the next day, the flags of truce being put up on several places, he went out to near old Tangier, where the Alcad of Titune[30] appointed him, our chief articles was to have the whole ground within Charles Fort and all our redouts for the use of the garrison, and to build within that pallisad at Folfort, which we had rendered ourselves masters of with our arms and with the loss of so much of our blood, with several others.

Talmash being with them till the evening, returned; he judged they might condescend to everything, except to the building within the pallisad: the next morning he went out and was with them till noone, they finding our general stuck to the building within the pallisad, they fell into a passion and abused the Jonas,[31] the interpreter, sadly, and said so long as there was a Moore, in Barbary they would not condescend to it; and told Lieut. Collonell Talmach sharply to return, for they would treat no more with us, and to cause take down the flaggs of truce, for they would immediately enter into war again: upon Talmach return with their answer, and the flaggs of truce being taken down, we fell immediately to hote fireing and lasted all, the rest of the day. That same night they began a trench from the old place of arms, before the fort, which advanced towards the pallisads on the right hand of the fort.

Two days after, they brought a piece of cannon to the place of arms before the fort, and made ane embrasor through the parapit, this coolled the courage of severalls. for Lieut. Coll. Sakvile having hopes of peace in that treatie, being disappointed, and Talmash and Major Bomlie being that night at supper in a tavern, fell a exclaiming against the proceedings during the war, with great heat and passion, and said he had always been against the undertakings of anything without that it was foolishly and rashly begun, and would certainly have a worse conclusion with reflecting upon Sir Pames conduct highly: this came to Sir Pames ears, and questioning him on it, he told Sir Pames that he

---

30. Tetuan.

31. Jonas, a renegade who had once been "Sexton's boy at Tangier." (*Routh.*)

had said nothing but what he would justify, and that if the king would make him governor he would not stay in Tangier.

And it is well known during all the time of his being there that it was frequently his subject, in all places to exclaim against the place, that it could never be made steadable to the king in no fashion, although there is several judicious men, that understands Tangier well, thinks that the charge and expence the king is at there might be better imployed in England, yet it was very unreasonable in him, who had the honour to command a battalion of guards, who should have given good example at that conjuncture, he and Talmach, their opinions running always together, became so uneasie to the governour that he did not know what to doe with them, but he judgeing them men that was supported with great interest at court, and he in hopes to have the commission to be governour, suffered patiently of them.

Some few days later Sir Jone Borie[32] passing with the Malligo fleet for England Lieut. Coll. Sakville and Talmash resolved, and disposed all their affairs, to goe aboard with Sir Jone Borie for England, and told they would not stay to see the tragicall conclusion of that war. Sir Pames finding them in earnest, sent and told them, if they continued longer their resolution, he would make them answer a council of war which stoped them. I cannot think with what a countenance they would a looked at court. The news come from Triff[33] that the two Spanish troops that was promised was there, waiting for us if we had need of them, upon which Sir Pames called a council of war of the field officers to have their opinions, Admiral Herbert did promote extreamely for sending for them,.

Mr. Shears was much against it with many arguments, but it was carryed that they should be sent for, and the ships ordered to sail and brought them good men well mounted and well commanded near the number of 200, the Moores having at this time advanced their trenches within 30 yards of the pallisad of the new work, and fearing they would [. . . .][34] beside they brought a trench upon the right hand of the fort round and within noro'd[35] redout, with a designe to cut off the communication between the fort and the town, it being now time to think upon what might be done for the defence of the place, the most part thinking it in a dangerous condition, the council of war was

---

32. Admiral Sir John Berry. See 'D.N.B,'
33. Tarifa.
34. An illegible word has been inserted here in the original.
35. Norwood.

called of the field officers, being assembled.

Sir Pames told it was to deliberat what was most fitting to be done for the defence of the place, whether or not ane outfall, Sakvile and Talmash with long harrangues and with strong arguments, as they believed, was against the outfall, several thinking it dangerous they believing the Moores armie strong; I told I did not believe the Moores was strong without, for several reasons and although they were both strong and formidable, my opinion was that it was very proper and necessare to undertake ane outfall, being their guards never appeard strong at their posts, and that the order of the outfall might be so disposed that we needed not risk too much the troops, in case the enemie come strong against us, and could not effectuate our designe in filling up their advanced trenches, and this I judged very necessare to be done in form for the defence of a place that had cost us so much blood in gaining, and that nothing might reflect upon us, then it was put to the vote, it was carried to make an outfall, but Sir Pames did not resolve on the day nor on the number of troops.

The next morning being Sunday Sir Pames drew out a detachment of 200 foot to an old work of the [. . . .][36] towards Charles Fort to make them cast up a breastwork there, there was a Spanish Captain and about 60 horsemen that was ordered to sustain the foot, Sir Pames in moveing about with Major Bekeman in ordering what should be done, Sir Pames received a shote in the body at a great distance and fell from his horse: he being brought in, and the news of his being killed, Lieut. Coll. Sakvile and I went to the Castle and found him in that condition that we judged he could not live long; Lieut. Coll. Sakevile falling to command in chiefe, it was fitting to move about to order what was necessare without, he and I went immediately to Peterburie Tower, to view the Moores and to see what effects it had, our men drawing out towards Charles Fort.

Major Bekeman having put those 200 men to work, this gave great jealousie to the Moores that we intended to Charles Fort again; this certainly brought all the force they had to that hand and to those trenches that cut off the communication betwixt the fort and the Castle; so that work had that good effects, that it gave us a full sight of all the force they had, which I judge was betwixt 2,000 and 3,000 men; this gave me the great assurance imaginable that we might done something considerable against them in our outfall, the Moores, seeing our men continued the working notwithstanding they had brought all

---

36. "Tivitt" has been inserted in original, *i.e.,* Teviot.

their force to that hand, they advanced most boldly out of the trenches with the most of their force exposed to our cannon and small shote, towards our workmen.

This put our men to their arms and the Spanish captain with his 60 horsemen seeing them advancing scatteredly and making constant fire he charged them most bravely home and beat them into their trenches again, he having lost several of his men and horse, he finding their fire hote on him retired, some of his men coming off precipitantly, our 200 men commanded be Captain Colgraffe, that before was at work having advanced to sustain the Spanish horse, upon the horse retiring, they most cowardly and basely run and left their officer, some few staying with the captain and the rest of the officers that came off safely, this was a shameful thing to see our foot misbehave at the rate when the Spaniard had done so well.

The next day soon in the morning I going to Polfort, I met Mr. Bekeman he told me that their trench from the old place of arms was advanced within 20 yards of the pallisad of the fort, and he said if we did not resolve very soon to make the outfall he would not set his foot again within the fort, for he judged they would advance again. I told him I had said all I could for the undertaking the outfall and I prayed him to speak again to Lieut. Coll. Sakville. Upon Mr. Bekeman's speaking to him he ordered a council of war to assemble of the field officers at admiral's house; being assembled, he said he had been always against the undertaking without, and especially that outfall for the reasons he had given, and now, the governour being past recoverie, he brought us together again to have an opinion about it. I told him that the outfall was resolved on before Sir Pames was wounded, and it would be a shameful thing for us to go back with it now, for the loss of one man: the Admiral and Major Bekeman being for it, with many good arguments, it was resolved on to be made, on Wednesday morning nixt, with all the force of the garrison, leaving only the ordinary guards within.

The next morning I went out betimes to the ground on the left hand of Polfort, where we designed to embattle the troops; after I had considered how to proceed against the enemy, with the best of my understanding, I went and found Lieut. Coll. Sakvile, and I prayed him to goe out to the rampart with me to shew him the designe I had in my head: after he understood the thing, he approved of it, and prayed me to meet him immediately after dinner to resolve upon everything that was necessare for the order of the thing, that the orders might be distribute to the commandants of the batallions at night after we had resolved on everything necessare for the designe and all things being disposed to the best advantage, that we judged for the next mornings work.

Being assembled we marched out the nixt morning be 3 a clock with the 7 troops of horse to the place of arms before Katrina Gate, where the troops of horse was ordered to halt, while the foot was a fileing out at an avenue at the foot of the line of communication to the fort, after our six battalions was near embattelled close on the left hand of the line, two battalions a front, our 7 troops being then drawn out and embattled on the left hand of the foot, being sufficiently covered on the right hand be the line and fort, we being so disposed in battle, as we judged most convenient for the designe in hand, and the situation of the ground, with a detachment of 50 men. Captain and Lieutenant, from each battalion, in six several platoons advanced for to make the first attack with an detachment of horse to sustain them [.... .][37] Admiral Herbert ordered all his long boats man'd with his sea-men to advance, as near to their battrie of 8 piece of cannon as they could, that was on the east of the town that play'd on the ships in the harbour, which proved of very good effect to us, for it made a diversion.

Macknie[38] troop with all the moll'd[39] horses with men mounted on them and some of our worst men with a great many collours and drums was ordered towards Charles Fort to give them allarum on that hand. Our detachments in plottoons being ordered to fall on to attack the several places that was designed, Captain Fittrie,[40] that commanded the detachment of guards with the half of the company of granadeers of Dumbarton's regiment commanded by Lieut Mak[41] having bravely advanced near to the place of arms where they had the piece of cannon, the enemy being strong in guard there, made great fire so that they killed several of the granadeers and of Fittrie's detachment so that the men did shrink and retire towards the fort, the 150 men that sallied out of Polfort commanded be Captain Londie[42] and

37. There is a blank space of two lines in original.
38. Captain Makenny, commanded one of the old troops of Horse at Tangier. *Routh.*
39. *i.e.*, the horses used for work on the Mole.
40. Captain Fawtrey (or Fortrey); commanded a company of the Duke of York's Regiment, in the King's Battalion.
41. A blank after Mak. in the original. Evidently Lieut. McCracken, of Dumbarton's. Lieutenant in April, 1679 (*Ormonde* MSS.) Captain of a newly raised Company in Dumbarton's, 22.9.1688. Served at Tangier, wounded 27.10.1680. Killed at Steenkirk, 1692. (*Regimental Records* and *Fortescue.*) A petition of 1703 states that Captain McCracken "signalised himself at Steenkirk by his management of cannon." (*Dalton.*)
42. Captain R. Lundy. See footnote 27.

Hommes[43] that was ordered to attack their advanced trench finding likewayes great resistance there and both the captain being wounded very soon in the beginning, and carried off, upon this the detachment retired towards the fort.

Our right hand being put in this condition meerly be the fault of the battalion of the guards that did not move at a fit distance with Fittrie's detachment to keep their men in countenance, I, who had charges and manadgement of the attack on the left hand their place of arms, at Monmouth Fort, with our 2 battallions and the battalion of seamen, I commanded Captain Melville[44] with his detachment and the other half of our company of granadeers to fall on and attack the place of arms, I moveing at a just distance to him with our battallions beside I prayed Captain Coy,[45] that was upon the left hand of all with his troop, to advance towards the place of arms at a soft[46] gallop, this encouraged our detachment so that they immediately fell in to the place of arms with the Moores, and the Moores seing our battalions so near with Coy's troop of horse they run so we was masters of it with little loss.

Captain Lakirt[47] who commanded the detachment of our first battalion seeing Captain Fattries men in disorder and likwayes the 150 men that sallied out of Polfort he very opportunely fell in upon their trench on the left hand of their piece of cannon in the place of arms, where they continued disputeing the business hotely till Lieut. Mack-

43. Captain George Hume of Dumbarton's. George Hume, Captain in Dumbarton's in April, 1679. (*Ormonde* MSS.) Commanded the Forlorn hope and was wounded, 14 May, 1680. Wounded again, 27 October, 1680. Did not embark with his company in 1684. Does not appear in any subsequent lists.

44. Patrick Melville. Captain in Dumbarton's in April, 1679. (*Ormonde* MSS.) Served at Tangier. Captain in 1684. Murdo McKenzie appointed (Captain, *vice* "late Pat. Melville," 1.10.1684. Barbara Melville, widow of late Captain Melville, of the Royal Foot, "died in the Service," awarded a pension of £30, in list of 1694-1700. (Dalton.)

45. Captain John Coy, commanding one of the six troops of Horse, raised by the Earl of Ossory in 1680, for service in Tangier, which eventually became the 1st Royal Dragoons. Coy had served in the Duke of Monmouth's Regiment of Horse and was subsequently Colonel of the 6th Horse (2nd Irish Horse), now the 5th D.Gs., 1688-97. He commanded a brigade of cavalry in Flanders, 1695-6. (*Dalton, Routh, Davis, Cannon*.)

46. Slow. See later where he speaks of "retiring softly."

47. Captain Julius Lockhart, of Dumbarton's. Appears as Lucius Lockhart in Ross's *Old Scottish Colours*. (Captain in 1679. (*Ormonde* MSS.) Second in Command of Forlorn Hope, 20.9.1680. Wounded 27.10.1680. Appears to have left the regiment in 1681, as Captain A. Urquhart replaced him.

rakrin who had keeped his granadeers together and seeing all things going well on the left hand at Monmouth fort he advanced again to the place of arms so near as to bestow his granads amongst them which he did liberally, and being followed with Captain Fattrie and them that sallied out of the fort advanced again, then the battallion of guards began to move.

Lieutenant Mackrakrin seing the disorder he had put amongst them with his granads fell in amongst them and being followed be Captain Fittrie the Moores run, and left our men masters of the place of arms, and the piece of cannon; the Moores that was beat from their several posts retired to James Fort having left many killed and wounded behind them, the Moores be this time having got all their force from their camp was betwixt James Fort and Sandhill Fort and in their trenches betwixt Sandhill Fort and Monmouth Fort, they being beat from their several posts where they keeped guard, I judged time to attack those trenches betwixt Monmouth Fort and Sandhill Fort with the first battallion of Dumbarton's regiment, being sustained with the second, they being numerous there and sustained with all their force, yet we very soon beatt them out of the first trench.

They retired without the old line betwixt Sandhill fort and Monmouth, and from that line they did gall us extreamely, we being near and exposed to their fire with whole bodie. I ordered our drums to beat the charge so that our battallions might move altogether in passing, we had great loss in passing that trench especially of our officers, passing first; so soon as we was over the trench with our battallion, the Moores run precipitantly from the outside of the old line, a sergeant of Captain Morrays[48] Company with some few soldiers passed the line, and fell in amongst the Moores, and took a colloures which was the first that was taken.

The first battalion of Insquine,[49] at the same time I attacked their trenches, entered in skirmish at some distance on our right hand, upon the advancing of a few Moores horse, the battallion brake and ran most shamefully, so that almost all the day after during the action there was no such thing to be found as the first battalion of Insquiny's Regimt., the second battallion of Insquiny, commanded be Captain Jailes seing things had succeeded well with us, they came up to the

---

48. Captain James Murray, of Dumbarton's.
49. William O'Brien, Earl of Inchiquin, 1638-92. Had served in France and Spain: and had been taken prisoner by corsairs and ransomed, *circa* 1660. Governor of Tangier, 1675-80. Governor of Jamaica, where he died 1692. (See 'D.N.B.')

line on our right hand near to the ruines of Sandhill Fort where the Moores retired that we had beat from the trenches [. . . .][50] they [. . . .][51] they had it hote being flanked from James Fort, the men beginning to wearie, Captain Jaile called to me and said he could not keep his men no longer, and asked me what he should doe: I ordered him to retire softly, and gave him great assistance of our officers to keep his men from running, which they had great inclination to doe; the Moores seing their battallion retire something precipitantlv followed them, horse and foot, close on their reere.

I had dispesed our battallions in the best order we could to take their ground, I advanced with our battallions and gave them a french[52] discharge, which stoped their pursute, and made them run to the ruines of sandhill fort again: the battallion of seamen, who was left on the line near Monmouth fort, they seeing the good success we had in beating the enemy from their trenches, they past over the line and moved to the east, over the sand hills, be this time near to the place of arms where the Moores had their piece of Cannon; Lieut. Coll. Sakville had caused fill up their trench for to make a passage for our horse, and ordered Don Salnedors[53], the commandant of the Spaniards, to pass with his troop, he designing no more of the horse to engage, Captain Nedbe[54] that was on the left hand near Monmouth fort with his troop, seeing the Spanish troop led over the trench be Lieut. Coll. Sakvile, he past the line near Monmouth Fort with his troop, and moved till he got on the head of the seamen; in this time we had disputed hotely with our two battalions of Dumbarton's with the Moores, that was posted about the mines of Sandhill Fort, till we beat them from thence, and was masters of the place.

Notwithstanding, they were sustained with all their force, and we being flanked from James Fort, which did gall us extreamly, so that our loss was very great above 250 soldiers and 24 officers of our two battallions, that was killed and wounded; if the battalion of the guards[55] had been so kind to us as to put themselves in the old line that goes

---

50. Words illegible in original.
51. Blank in original.
52. ? fresh.
53. Don Salvador de Monforte.
54. Charles Neatby, or Needby. Had served in Monmouth's Regiment of Horse and commanded at Tangier one of the six Troops raised by the Earl of Ossory in 1680, which eventually became 1st Royal Dragoons.
55. O.C. King's Battn., "although strongly urged by his officers, refused to move to support of the Scots." (*Hamilton.*)

from the place of arms to James Fort, they might a made our work much easier, and cheaper to us, which might a done without exposeing themselves, but they judged it safer for them to continue within the place of arms: so soon as I was master of the ruines of Sandhill Fort, I found still our battallions was much exposed to the enemies fire from James Fort.

I judged absolutely necessare either to retire to have some covert, or to undertake to beat them from James Fort; and finding our men still in heart, notwithstanding the great loss we had and I seing Lieut. Coll. Sakevile and Don Salledore with his troop advancing towards us, which gave us assurance, I moved to James Fort with our battallions where the most of the enemies force was, with several collours; the Moores seing us and the troop of horse advancing and Captain Nedbe that was in pursute some scattered Moores over the sandhills towards their camp, they ran without makeing great resistance there to all hands.

So soon as I can the length of James Fort with our two battallions, I see the Moores pulling off a small brass piece of cannon towards their camp, and finding the Moores running precipitantly to all hands I passed the old line at James Fort, I seing but very few horse of the enemy in the field, and beat them from their cannon, and I charged our aid-major to cause pull in the cannon towards Polfort; be this time Lieut. Coll. Sakevile with Don Sallnedo's troop was come the length of James Fort, and seeing the Moores running, he was ordered to charge them that was running towards their camp, he very deliberatly for some time looked about him, till he saw Captain Nedbe almost into their camp in pursute of them, then he at a good brisk gallop charged, where they convoyed the Moores the length of their camp, in makeing all the way very good use of their swords the Moores having thrown away their arms in their camp; he mett with Captain Nedbe and his troop that had made good use of his time, then they thought it fitt to retire.

Captain Nedbe having taken two colloures, one with his own hands; and Don Galinedos one colloures, so they came off with very little loss: some few of our foot out of greed of plunder stole from our battallions, went too far out, where some was killed: after the 2 troop of horse retired again within the old line, I was posted with our two battallions at James Fort and near it all the rest of the day, till 5 a clock, where I continued in skirmish with the enemie, that had the confidence to return again with their collours after so considerable a loss as they had, and we having made a full discoverie of their force, which was remarkable after all their trenches was filled up all round Polfort and a little addition to Polfort, we resolved to retire into town so this days work past much hapilyer than the most part believed, although our loss was great, which was well timed and well enough designed, and most bravely be a part of the troops, but the great fault of all was that all our troops of horse was not suffered to engadge, which if they had they would certainly given an account of all the Moores that they had before the town, for the Moores prisoners that was taken in the action said their armie consisted of about 3,000 men, there did not appear so many in the action and not above a 100 horse.

The next day Lieut. Coll. Sakvile sent them out their dead bodies that was killed within our old lines, their loss was great but they believed it much greater than it was, as they confessed themselves, for there deserted many of their men so that they did not know, whither they were killed or not, and they were certainly very much discouraged with their defeat, for there appeared no Moores for 3 or 4 days after near the town: till that the Alcad Domar returned to them, for he was not at the action, for it was the Alcad of Titoune that commanded them, at his return he found his armie extreamely discouraged and diminished, yet he resolved to put a good countenance on, as you may judge be this short letter that he wrote to Sir Pames, believing he was still alive, as it was interpret so:

> I arrived here yesternight and I have heard of your action Wednesday last which I believe was not cheap to neither of us, and likewayes that you most cruelly caused murder many of our men in cold blood, after you took them into town, if this be true I would have no more dealling with you, now you know I am here and that the war is not yet at ane end.

I was at Lieut. Coll. Sakevile's Chamber when he received this letter, he shewed concernment; and when it was read, he with several others that believed that the Alcad Domar was so proud and ambitious a man and could command what force he pleased would be more incensed than discouraged with the late defeat, and would think upon nothing but revenge; I told Coll. Sakevile, at that same time, there being nobody by, that certainly the *alcad* had write this letter to show a good countenance, and that it was not to be believed they could continue long before the town, or get more force, considering that it is now the season that they butt of necessity to labour their ground, and that there never presented so good ane occasion to have ane honourable and advantagious peace as now.

The next day after, the *alcad* wrote a letter to Admiral Herbert, the substance of it was in complaining of my Lord Insequine and Sir Pames that they had several times broke their word to him, and that he could not confide in them, and that he would enter into a treatie of peace with him; now they are the first that makes the offer of peace, and showed ane earnest desire to goe about it soon, so that in reason we might expected of them what they refused before to Sir Pames; after, the admiral sent his answer to the *alcad*, and told he commanded only the king's fleet and that there was a necessity he behoved to treat with the governour.

Then the nixt day Lieut. Coll. Sakevile caused draw a letter to send to the *alcad* to this purpose,—he told that Sir Pames was dead, and that our loss was very considerable in the late action, and that he succeeded to the government, and had full power from the king to treate for a lasting peace with them, and that he would send out an ambassadour. He sent this letter to the admiral, to know whether he approved of it to be sent, the admiral sent him word he did not approve of the letter; yet, notwithstanding, he sent immediately the letter to the *alcad*, now any reasonable man may judge that this letter would be very agreeable to the *alcad*; it was necessare to tell them that Sir Pames was dead, because he behoved to treate in his own name; but why to tell them that our loss was considerable, I cannot tell, unless it was to appease the *alcad* that he judged was so bent on revenge, the *alcad* without difficulty would conclude that Sir Pames was killed in the last action and would say to his officers that was much discouraged with their late defeat, and wearied of the war, that certainly we was more discouraged with our loss than they with theirs, as appeared plainly by our governour's letter, so we found the effect of Sakevile's letter for the nixt morning we found all the Moores force again posted round as near as they could.

Then Lieut. Col. Sakevile ordered a councill of war to he at the admiral's lodgeing to have our opinions concerning the cessation of arms, he representing how well it would relish with the king to have a peace at any condition at that conjuncture of time, everyone was of the opinion ane occasion to have so honourable and so advantagious a peace as then, and to have a care that there was not bad preparative made, since the king's ambassador was expected every day to land, who had the king's instructions concerning the peace, and my Lord

Plimouth's Regiment[56] with 200 recruits to my Lord Dumbarton's Companies which was a considerable reinforce to a garrison after they had beat the enemy in the fields, and that we judged it better to continue in fortifying of Polfort, which the Moores durst not offered to hinder us, and not to precipitate in the treatie, but wait the ambassador's coming, and the forces that he knew was on the way; if the Moores would not condescend to what we might justly expected: but Lieut. Coll. Sakvile, finding our opinions differ from his own, he resolved to consult us no more, and would have all the honour of the management of the treatie to himself and Mr. Shears, who was his only counsellor; so he made choice of Mr. Beather, who is no sojer and sent him out with his instructions to the *alcad*.

The *alcad* in the beginning believed there was some cheat in the business, finding things so easie and we so bent on the peace, but at last he found Lieut. Coll. Sakevile in good earnest, so that what be threatenings and be fair promises, when the ambassadors came, that all the countrey as far out as we pleased should be at our service so that he brought our unable and timerous managers to what he pleased.

I cannot but wonder extreamely at Lieut. Coll. Sakevile who is a man of so little service and experience in the wars, how he durst adventure to go on in a treatie, without the advice of the admiral and officers of service, and to condescend to such dishonourable and disadvantagious things, as the paying of powder and arms yearly, and other expensive things to the king, to an enemie to make such a preparative when he was sure he could have had a cessation of arms till the king's ambassador came over, and the forces, that had landed some four or 5 days after, that he had concluded and agreed everything with the *alcad*, and some few days after Sir James Lesley[57] landed who was sent ambassador from the king, and he finding his business almost quite spoiled by the bad preparative that our timerous and unable manager of the peace had made in condescending to such mean and disadvantageous things especially after a victory, which has certainly made the Moores believe that the king will condescend to anything rather than to enter to war with them.

Sir James, who was always imployed in all the business of trea-

---

56. The 2nd Tangier Regiment; in 1922 "The King's Own Royal Regiment (Lancaster)."

57. Captain James Leslie, had served as cornet in a troop of Horse at Tangier, in 1664. Was appointed Major in Tangier Regiment of Foot 1680, and Lieut.-Colonel in 1687. Was knighted when appointed ambassador to the Moors. Surrendered Dixmude in 1695, for which he was cashiered. (*Routh. Dalton*. I. 177.)

ties with the Moores, and understands well what they are, he had yet thoughts to going it about so as to have a lasting peace upon more advantageous terms, than what was condescended to. Lieut.Coll. Sakevile preceiving his designe, who thought it would be a great reflection on him that anything should be mended or bettered that he had condescended to. he then puts it to Sir James Lesley, to sign that agreement that he had made with the Alcad Domar, Sir James who found so many disadvantageous things in it, he excuses himself that he was not present in the time of the war, nor in the time of the treatie, this made Mr. Shears and Lieut. Collonell Kirk[58] and those that had signed that agreement to be Sir James enemie, so that they endeavoured to diminish his credit with the King of Morroco and the *alcad*

Lieut. Coll. Sakvile wrote over that they were not satisfied with Sir James being sent embassadour, because he was not of quality enough, so that he would be obliged to send Lieut. [59] Kirk to the emperor before Sir James went, a very prettie invention indeed for the Moores has not so much that distinction of quality amongst them as any other nation has, and Sir James told me himself, when he came to the emperor's court he could very well have mended that agreement that Sakvile had made, if it had not been Lieut. Coll. Kirk that hindered it, so it proved that Sakevile's ambassador had more credit there than the king's; so Sir James had not much more to doe but to deliver the king's presents to the emperor, upon which the emperor complemented Sir James with the quiteing of that article which obliged the king to pay so many bolls[60] of cloath yearly.

Now if Lieut. Coll. Sakeville finds this reflect highly upon him, and say that there is no truth in what I say, I advise him to tell the king that he had the good fortune to be at the head of one of the prettiest actions that has been done since the king's restauration, and yet I who served under his command does say and will prove he deserves to loss his head for his management there, for he opposed everything that was right designed and for the good of the place, and certainly it concerns his Majestie's Service to go to the bottome of this, to make a distinction betwixt those that served him well and ill.

Now what I have observed or can learn concerning the Moores

---

58. The well-known Colonel Percy Kirke, of the old Tangier Regiment, now "The Queen's Royal Regiment (West Surrey)"—known as Kirke's Lambs. See 'D.N.B.'
59. Lieut.-Colonel.
60. An old Scots dry measure, generally used for grain, potatoes, etc. A boll of canvas was 36 yards.

is, that they cannot maintain a considerable army before Tangier for several reasons; for their prince gives no pay, nor can not for they have little or no comerce with Christendom, their countrey is waste, without villages, so that soldiers can get nothing wherewithal to subsist, their towns is far separat, and not populous from whence he has his soldiers, and obey him far more for fear than love. The mountaneers is not at his command, for they run betwixt him and his nevoy,[61] as they find things uneasie to them, and shuns all occasions of going to the wars.

I have seen the strongest army they have had before Tangier since the king has had the place; the greatest number at a time was when the Earle of Tiviot was a building Charles Fort, and certainly would give them as much jealousie as anything, that Christians should enlarge themselves in their country, so that Galland did bring all the force that possibly he could bring against the town which I judge was betwixt three or four thousand men.

Here the MSS. ends abruptly.

---

61. ? nephew.

Historical Record of the Second or Queen's Royal Regiment of Foot

Richard Cannon

The Second Regiment of Foot was raised in 1661, for the purpose of providing a garrison for Tangier, a fortress on the northern coast of Africa, which was ceded to England as part of the marriage portion of Donna Catherina, Infanta of Portugal, who, in the following year, was married to King Charles II. (See note following).

★★★★★

Note:—The marriage portion of Queen Catherine included the city of Tangier, the Island of Bombay, and a sum equal to 300,000*l.* sterling. Tangier is a place of great antiquity, and was formerly one of the most splendid cities in Africa. It is stated by Procopius Caesariensis to have been founded by the Phoenicians; it was known by the name of *Tingis*, or *Tinja*, and was taken by the Romans under Sertorius. It was afterwards captured by the Vandals, and was retaken by the celebrated Belisarius, who restored it to Justinian. On the invasion of the Saracens it was surrendered to them by Count Julian. In the fifteenth century it was the scene of several desperate engagements between the Moors and Portuguese; and in 1437 Prince Ferdinand was defeated before the city, and his army subjected to an ignominious capitulation. In 1471 it was taken by Alfonso V., king of Portugal. After the death of Sebastian, it fell into the hands of Spain; but upon the restoration of the Braganza family to the throne of Portugal, in 1640, it was once more annexed to that monarchy.

★★★★★★

The command of this regiment was conferred by King Charles II. on Henry (second) Earl of Peterborough, whose commission as colonel bears date the 30th of September, 1661.

King Charles II. having, soon after his restoration, disbanded the army of the Commonwealth, the ranks of Lord Peterborough's regiment were speedily completed with disciplined soldiers: it is reported to have assembled on Putney heath on the 14th of October, 1661, and to have numbered one thousand men.

The destination of Lord Peterborough's regiment to garrison so valuable a portion of Her Majesty's dower was, no doubt, the cause of its early advancement to royal favour: it was designated 'the Queen's' and the *Paschal Lamb*, the distinguishing badge of Portugal, was placed on its colours, and has ever since been continued to be borne by the regiment.

In a few months after its formation, the Earl of Peterborough embarked with his regiment and a troop of horse,[1] and arrived at Tangier on the 29th of January, 1662, where he found a British fleet, under the command of the Earl of Sandwich, lying in the roads, and Sir Richard Steyner, with a detachment of officers and seamen, occupying the town: a duty from which the Queen's Regiment relieved them on the following day[2].

COPY OF A LETTER ADDRESSED BY KING CHARLES II.:—

To the Earl of Peterborough.

Dated Whitehall, y. 21st of 10^{ber} 1661. My Lord Peterborough:—I am very well satisfied of your care and dilligence in the employment your are in, for which I thank you very heartily. And assure yourself I have so just a sense of this and all your other services, as you shall find upon all occasions how much I esteem and value all those who serve me faithfully. I have noe more to adde at present only to desire you to lett those honest men knowe who are along with you, yet they shall allwayes be in my particular care and protection, as persons yet venture themselves in my service. And so wishing you a good voyage I remain

Your very affectionate friend

Charles R.

The fortress was already surrounded by walls upwards of a mile and

---

1. Bibl. Harl., 6844.
2. *Mercurius Publicus.*

a quarter in extent, but the English began constructing, at immense cost both of money and labour, a series of external fortifications. It was also determined to form a secure harbour by building a pier, or mole, several hundred yards in length. A spirit of enterprise, which has since become so conspicuous in British subjects, was, at this early period, strongly evinced in these improvements, carried on amidst barbarian tribes on the unpromising shores of Africa.

Tangier was announced after its occupation 'a place of such concernment that all the world will envy the English the attainment of it;' but this opinion was founded more on an expectation that the new colony would open a mart for trade, and bring to our influence, if not to our power, the adjoining states. It was, however, an acquisition of consequence to a nation aiming at commercial rivalry at a time when the voyage to India by the Cape of Good Hope was of rare occurrence. Tangier was situated so as to be a convenient resting-place for the Mediterranean trader, similar to what Gibraltar affords at the present time. These speculations gave the command a great importance, made evident by the warrant from King Charles II. on the appointment of the Earl of Peterborough to his government. It designates him:

> Captain General, Chief Governor, and Vice-Admiral of our City of Tangier, and of the ports and coasts adjacent, and any of our dominions and territories, castles and forts, in or near the kingdom of Tangier, Fez, and Morocco, in Africa, which are or shall be in our possession, or reduced to our obedience, &c.

On the arrival of Lord Peterborough at Tangier, he found Gaylan, the sovereign chief of Fez, with a body of 10,000 men, encamped within a league of the fortress. A treaty of peace was concluded between these commanders, and limits were fixed, beyond which the English were not to forage or cultivate. No great reliance was placed by the British on their new ally, and accounts from the new colony state, 'how the Moors will observe these articles we know not; however, we are, and we still shall be, upon our guard.'

Three other battalions of infantry also proceeded to Tangier from Dunkirk.[3] The friendly understanding which was established with the

---

3. These battalions were part of the royal force which fought for Charles I. during the civil war in England. In 1657 they entered the service of Spain; and in 1660 were placed in garrison at Dunkirk; in 1663 they were incorporated in the Queen's Tangier Regiment. Dunkirk had been taken from the Spaniards by the combined armies of England and France in 1658, and was ceded in 1659 to England. It was sold by King Charles II. to the French, for 500,000*l.*

natives was for some time interrupted only by trifling skirmishes, in which the Moors satisfied themselves by beating back, with sticks, those of the garrison who passed the stipulated bounds. A jealousy was, however, very soon evinced; and upon opposition being made to the English in prosecuting the works and fortifications already alluded to, war burst out, in which the number and ferocity of the Moors were defeated and overcome by great discipline and courage on the part of the garrison. The use of cannon by the Europeans at length diminished the courage of the barbarians, but not before the garrison suffered severely. They had already lost 250 men, and the Moors about 500, amongst whom was a brother of Gaylan, when a peace was at length concluded in 1663, and Lord 1663 Peterborough returned in the same year to England. (See note following).

★★★★★★

Note:—Henry, Lord Mordaunt, second Earl of Peterborough was the son and heir of John, first Earl of Peterborough, who died in 1642. He raised a regiment, at his own expense, in behalf of King Charles I.; was wounded at the Battle of Newbury on the 27th of October, 1644, and in 1648 was concerned, with the Earl of Holland, in an attempt to rescue the king from his imprisonment:—the Earl of Holland was taken, and was beheaded in February, 1649; the Earl of Peterborough, and big brother John, (who was created Lord Mordaunt and Viscount Avelon on the 10th of July, 1659.) escaped, and were voted traitors to the Commonwealth, and their estates were sequestered, The services of the Earl of Peterborough, in support of the royal cause, during the civil wars, entitled him to the favour of King Charles II. at the Restoration; and the colonelcy of the Queen's regiment of foot, and the governorship of Tangier, were deservedly conferred upon a nobleman who, under the severest trials of his fortitude and consistency, had shown himself a constant and zealous supporter of monarchical government. He was employed in several important situations of trust in the service of King James II., and on the 20th of June, 1685, he was appointed colonel of the 3rd Regiment of Horse, (now the 2nd Dragoon Guards,) from which he was removed at the Revolution in 1688. His lordship died on the 19th of June, 1697, and was succeeded in his titles, &c, by his nephew, Charles, third Earl of Peterborough, so celebrated in the wars in

✶✶✶✶✶✶

The Earl of Peterborough was succeeded, both in the government of Tangier and in the colonelcy of the Queen's Regiment, by Lieutenant-General Andrew Rutherford, Earl of Teviot (late Governor of Dunkirk), whose commission was dated the 9th of April, 1663. This second governor of Tangier consolidated all the infantry in garrison, and added them to the Queen's Tangier Regiment; he also so beautified and strengthened the town, that he obtained the title of its 'Restorer.'

Gaylan, hearing of the progress of the works, assembled an army of 4000 horse and 20,000 foot[4]; and at mid-day, on Sunday the 14th of June, 1663, when all the officers were at dinner, the Moors surprised and carried the advance-posts and attacked the great redoubt, where Major Ridgert of the Queen's Regiment, with forty men, made a most gallant defence, until the garrison, led by Colonel Norwood, sallied out, and charging the Moors with signal bravery, retook all the posts which had been captured. The garrison lost fourteen men killed and twenty wounded in this encounter; and the enemy upwards of one hundred. In an account of this action published at the time, it is stated:

> The Moors are men of resolution, and have most excellent fire-arms. When the horse charged us, he that did command them was clothed in crimson velvet, who being killed, they all went off immediately; it is presumed, therefore, that he was one of their chief men.

A second attack was subsequently made with 10,000 men:

> But the most vigilant governor had so warily supplied the defects of the place, by planting great guns to annoy the assailants, that though the assault was very sharp, the enemy was beaten off with the loss of 900 men.[5]

In August a peace was concluded for six months, and a free trade was opened with the Moors, 'they daily bringing their camels laden with commodities, and in return they get money and other things.' Further additions were also made to the works, which again gave rise to acts of hostility, and in one encounter the garrison captured a splen-

4. *History of Tangier*, published by authority in 1664.
5. *Ibid.*

did scarlet standard. A correspondence was opened with Gaylan—the Earl of Teviot insisted on making additional works—Gaylan objected, when his Lordship replied, 'he must have peace on those terms, or war without them.' The latter was the result, and led to numerous losses, particularly of the natives, in attempts to assault the fortress.

The chief losses sustained by the garrison of Tangier 1664 were in the sallies they made into the adjacent country to obtain fresh provisions. The Moors had a custom of driving two or three hundred head of cattle within sight of the walls, and planting a body of men in ambuscade, ready to fall on the detachment, which military ardour, to say nothing of a natural wish for fresh beef, was sure to bring beyond the cover of the fortress. These skirmishes frequently brought on more serious engagements, and in a sally made by the garrison on the 4th of May, 1664, the Earl of Teviot[6] met his death.

The Earl of Teviot was succeeded in the command of the Queen's Regiment by Colonel, afterwards Lieutenant-General Henry Norwood, whose commission is dated the 10th of June, 1664. The government of Tangier at this time was bestowed by His Majesty on John Lord Bellasyse, a younger son of the Earl of Fauconberg, who arrived at his government in April 1665, on board the Smyrna fleet, consisting of 'seven lusty, brave ships'

Lord Bellasyse found the judicious arrangements of the late commander-in-chief had rendered Tangier impregnable to its enemies, who by this time were much disheartened, and inclined to terminate hostilities. A peace was concluded in the following year, and Lord Bellasyse was himself the bearer of it to England, where he arrived in May, 1666, The *London Gazette* states his favourable reception by His Majesty, and great expectations of future prosperity to Tangier were raised from his report.

General Norwood, who has been mentioned as succeeding, on the

---

6. Andrew Rutherford, Earl of Teviot, was of a Scotch family, and he commanded a battalion of Scots Guards in the French service for several years. He attained the rank of Lieutenant-General, in France, and enjoyed considerable reputation for his military talents. At the Restoration he accompanied King Charles II to England, and having been especially recommended to the notice of his sovereign by Louis XIV., was created, in 1661, Lord Rutherford. He was appointed, on the 22nd of May, 1661, to succeed Sir Edward Harley as Governor of Dunkirk, which he held until the place was sold and delivered up to the French in 1662: on the 2nd of February, 1663, he was advanced to the dignity of Earl of Teviot. He was killed in an engagement with the Moors on the 4th of May, 1664, as above stated; and dying without issue, his title became extinct.

Divers Prospects in and about
TANGIER.
Exactly delineated by Wᵐ Hollar, his Maᵗⁱᵉˢ
designer, A 1669. and by him afterwards
to satisfie the curious, etchd in Copper.
And are to be sold by John Overton at the
white Horse without Newgate London.

Prospect of yᵉ North side of Tangier regarding the supine Sea.   From the hull as you come from Whitby or the Works toward the Towne

death of the Earl of Teviot, to the command of the Queen's Regiment, was now appointed to succeed Lord Bellasyse in his government. His administration was that of a judicious and vigilant officer; he acquired the confidence of the Moors, and conciliated Gaylan the sovereign chief of Fez. General Norwood's proceedings among the natives were considered so honourable, and his character, altogether, stood so high, that the Emperor Muley Xeriff admitted him to traffic at Tetuan free of imposts; a most beneficial offer, which he failed not to accept, as it so much concerned the welfare of Tangier, 'to whose advancement,' says Addison, 'he always declared a singular propensity.'

The death of this valuable officer, which occurred in 1668, made room for the appointment of John Earl of Middleton, whose commission, us Governor of Tangier, and as Colonel of the Queen's Regiment, is dated the 15th of May, 1668.

It was during the colonelcy of the Earl of Middleton, when war had been resumed with the ferocious Moors, that this regiment had the honour of numbering amongst its volunteers the man who afterwards became the most successful and most celebrated general of his age;—'the man who never fought a battle which he did not gain, or besieged a town which he failed to reduce,—John Churchill, Duke of Marlborough.'[7] Mr. Churchill 1668 was at this time about twenty years of age, and held an ensign's commission in the Foot Guards, but made his first essays, in actual service, beneath the walls of Tangier, where he eagerly engaged in the frequent sallies and skirmishes of the garrison, giving, in this desultory warfare, the first indication of his active and daring character.

After an administration of nearly seven years, the Earl of Middleton died in the fortress, on the 25th of January, 1675.[8] He was succeeded in the command of Tangier, and also in the colonelcy of the Queen's Regiment, on the 5th of March, 1675, by William O'Brien, Earl of Inchiquin.

Tangier had by this time so increased in strength and importance, that its occupation by the English was become an object of jealousy,

---

7. *Marlborough's Wars* 1 (1702-1707) and *Marlborough's Wars* 2 (1707-1709) are also published by Leonaur.

8. The Earl of Middleton who was appointed Governor of Tangier, was John, first Earl, so celebrated in the History of Scotland during the civil wars, and in the early years of King Charles's Restoration. He had been deprived, in 1663, of all his offices, and received the governorship of Tangier as a kind of honourable exile. Charles, second Earl of Middleton, his son, followed the fortunes of the House of Stuart, and his estate was forfeited by Act of Parliament, 1695.

not only to the natives of the country, but to all European powers. The fortifications had been rendered secure, and the harbour had been improved, and now afforded a safe anchorage. These important points had not been attained without great opposition from the Moors, and much credit was given to the garrison for their conduct and steady perseverance in the arduous duties they had to perform. We find acknowledgment made of them by the journals of the day in the following terms:—

> Many and various have been the warlike exploits of the heroic English against the barbarians, during the possession of this famous garrison of Tangier, so much renowned throughout the world, standing as commandress of those seas, and a protection to shipping from the Turkish pirates.

The *Oxford Gazette* of the same period also contains a letter from Tangier, reporting a threatened attack from a French fleet, and adds, 'the soldiers, far from being surprised at the news, are infinitely rejoiced at it, expecting them with much impatience.' Thus we find the Queen's Regiment was ever at its post, and had for eighteen years, almost single-handed, maintained this important fortress, in defiance of numerous assaults from the equally destructive effects of war and climate.

Towards the termination of the Earl of Inchiquin's[9] command in 1680, Tangier became an object of still greater attention in England. The Emperor of Morocco had joined with the forces of Fez, and a crusade was carrying on against the Christian occupants of this part of Africa; Europeans were found ready to direct the operations of the savages, and the war assumed an importance hitherto not bestowed on it. The following is an account given at the time:—

---

9. William O'Brien, second Earl of Inchiquin, served under his father in Catalonia, and in other foreign wars, during which, being ordered to command the troops sent to assist the Portuguese in their revolt from Spain, he and his father, with all the family, were taken by an Algerine *corsair*. In this engagement he lost his eye by a shot. In 1675 he was appointed Captain General of His Majesty's Forces in Africa, and Governor and Vice-Admiral of the Royal Citadel of Tangier, and of the adjacent parts, in which government he continued six years. In 1688 he was attainted by King James's Parliament, and had his estate sequestered; during which troubles he headed a considerable body of Protestants in Munster, who, being surprised by Major-General M'Carthy, were all disarmed. After the Revolution, he was made Governor of Jamaica and Vice-Admiral of the seas thereof; in which island he lived sixteen months only after his arrival. He died in January, 1691, at St. Jago de la Vega.

The Moors being vexed, knowing it was impossible to make their approaches against Tangier above ground, resolved to effect it by drawing lines and working underneath the earth; which stratagem of war, it is supposed, they learnt from several French and Spanish mercenaries whom they keep in pay: this practice they were before quite ignorant of.

The public journals also speak indignantly of some English who clandestinely imported 1500 barrels of gunpowder to the enemy, and say:

'Tis too often the custom of our nation to give away their swords, and fight with their teeth, and furnish our foes with means to cut our own throats.

Numerous losses sustained by the garrison, together with the increased force of the assailants, rendered it requisite to send reinforcements to the relief of the former. For this purpose a detachment left Ireland in the spring of 1680, consisting of four companies of the Royal Regiment of Foot; twelve other companies of the same regiment followed in the same year; five companies of the Foot Guards also sailed for the same destination under the Earl of Mulgrave.

In addition to the above reinforcements, a new regiment was raised in 1680, of which Charles Fitz Charles, Earl of Plymouth, (a natural son of King Charles II.) was appointed Colonel, and embarked on this service. This latter corps was called 'the Second Tangier Regiment,' and is now the 4th, or King's Own Regiment.

It has been stated that the Duke of Marlborough was initiated at Tangier in the first rudiments of war. The same theatre for the display of British valour and enterprise was at this time chosen by several other volunteers, among whom were Charles Lord Mordaunt, the afterwards celebrated Earl of Peterborough, and others of rank and celebrity.

In the year 1680 the Earl of Inchiquin vacated his appointment on being made Governor of Jamaica. Colonel Sir Palmes Fairborne,[10] of the Queen's Regiment, who succeeded to the command of the fortress on the departure of the Earl of Inchiquin, was, in consequence of

10. Sir Palmes Fairborne was son of Colonel Stafford Fairborne, of Nottinghamshire. He served as a soldier of fortune at the siege of Candia. There is a monument to his memory in Westminster Abbey, with a long and elegant inscription, in verse, from the pen of Dryden. His son, Sir Stafford Fairborne, was an admiral in the reigns of King William and Queen Anne.

his gallant and meritorious services, confirmed in the appointment by his Majesty. The demise of this brave officer, however, occurred before the commission for his appointment was signed; he was wounded in an action with the Moors on the 24th of October, 1680, and died three days after, leaving the charge of the garrison to Lieutenant-Colonel Edward Sackville, of the Coldstream Foot Guards.[11]

On the 27th of October the garrison attacked the enemy's lines with determined bravery, and the Queen's Regiment is reported to have 'behaved to admiration.'[12] Considerable loss was however sustained by the English:

'Not above fifty men were left in one of the battalions of Lord Inchiquin's Regiment (the Queen's): the English and Scotch behaved as brave and gallant men, and the Gentlemen Volunteers have alike proved themselves men of courage.'

The Queen's Regiment had Ensign Watson, Ensign Trent, and thirty-four men killed; and Captain Philpot, Lieutenants Guy and Tate, Ensigns Roberts, Thomas, Fitzpatrick, Webster, Norwood, Beckford, and Elliott, with 124 men wounded.

In a short period after the above engagement, his 1681 Majesty was pleased to appoint Lieutenant-Colonel Sackville to be Lieutenant-Colonel of the Queen's Regiment of Foot Guards, by which he was removed from service at Tangier.

The Government of Tangier was next conferred upon 1682 Colonel Piercy Kirke,[13] who, on the death of the Earl of Plymouth, had been promoted, on the 27th of November 1680, to the Colonelcy of the 2nd Tangier Regiment, with which regiment he had embarked

11. Lieutenant-Colonel Sackville was promoted to the rank of Colonel on the 12th of June, 1685; of Brigadier-General on the 3rd of July, 1685; and of Major-General on the 7th of November, 1688. He gave up his commissions to King James II. on the 19th of December, 1688.

12. *Narrative of the Great Engagement at Tangier*, 1680.

13. Colonel Piercy Kirke had served under the Duke of Monmouth in the army of the King of France, by the special permission of HIS Majesty King Charles II., granted on the 23rd of February, 1673: he was Captain Lieutenant of the Earl of Oxford's own troop of the Royal Regiment of Horse Guards in 1675, and was promoted from that regiment to be Lieutenant-Colonel of the Earl of Plymouth's, or the 2nd Tangier Regiment, (now the 4th Foot) on its being raised in 1680, and he embarked with it for Tangier in September of that year. Having distinguished himself in several actions with the Moors, on the death of the Earl of Plymouth at Tangier, he was promoted to the Colonelcy of the 2nd Tangier Regiment on the 27th of November, 1680, and was transferred to the Queen's Regiment on the 19th of April, 1682.

for Africa as Lieutenant-Colonel in September of that year. He was removed to the Colonelcy of the Queen's Regiment on the 19th of April, 1682, in succession to Colonel Sir Palmes Fairborne, deceased.

During Colonel Kirke's services at Tangier, he had been frequently employed upon missions to the Emperor of Morocco. In Ockley's *Account of South-west Barbary*, there is a letter from the emperor to him, dated the 27th of October, 1682, which shows that there was a mutual interchange of civilities between them; it is written to acknowledge the receipt of a present of three English horses, which, however thankful he might be, the emperor seems to think might have been improved upon, for he remarks, 'everybody knows that a carriage requires *four* horses to travel.'

The support of the colony of Tangier appears to have been a matter of serious dispute between the king and the Parliament: repeatedly the king urged upon the House of Commons the importance of the place, and the House as often acknowledged it; but still withheld the supplies necessary for its defence.

The advantage derived from the Levant trade, the fact that two millions of money had been expended on the works, and various arguments in favour of maintaining Tangier, were at length fully set forth in a speech from His Majesty on the 17th of November, 1680: a reply was made to it in eighteen articles, but the following remarks will sufficiently explain the whole affair, and account for the final sacrifice of the colony:—

It was said by the Parliament that the money granted for works had been misapplied;—that the same thing might happen again; and although they were, indeed, afraid of Tangier, they were more afraid of a popish successor.—It was a nursery, not only for popish soldiers, but also for priests and religious persons too, and that there had been sometimes a popish governor of the place, so that to succour it was but to augment their present evils.

In December, 1680, and again, in a Royal Declaration, dated the 8th of April, 1681, its great importance was urged. At length, in 1683, the king, finding the expense of maintaining the garrison and fortifications greater than he was willing, or, unassisted by Parliament, able to bear, came to the resolution of recalling the one, and demolishing the other.

About the end of the year 1683, Admiral Lord Dartmouth was

sent to Tangier with twenty sail of the line, with orders to demolish the fortress and mole, and to bring away the inhabitants and garrison. Great sufferings had been endured for some time for want of supplies from England, and much joy was evinced by the former on the announcement being made. In six months all the arrangements to abandon this once favourite colony being completed, the final evacuation took place in April, 1684. The Portuguese Government had offered a remuneration to have Tangier restored to that nation, but their power of defending it was questionable, and it was not considered prudent to risk so important a fortress falling into the hands of the Moors.

There are no means of ascertaining the number of officers and men lost by the Queen's Regiment during the twenty-two years of its service at Tangier; but to judge from the casualties amongst officers of superior rank, it must have been immense. The regiment had steadily persevered in performing the arduous duties required of it, and now retired from its post when a final evacuation of the fortress took place, by the king's command.

The Queen's Regiment left Tangier in April, 1684; and on its arrival in England it mustered 560 men, who were portioned into 16 companies. This number was part of 2300 troops, which had comprised the garrison of Tangier, and which, beside the Queen's Regiment, included

4 Troops of horse, which were incorporated in the Royal Dragoons.

5 Companies of Foot Guards.

16 Companies of Earl of Dumbarton's (now 1st or Royal Regiment).

16 Companies Trelawny's 2nd Tangier Regiment (now 4th or King's Own).

1 Company of Miners.

4 Independent Companies.

History of the First or Royal Regiment of Foot

Richard Cannon

Soon after the arrival of the regiment from France, a number of men, who each carried a large pouch filled with Hand-Grenades, were added to the establishment, and formed into a company, under the command of Captain Robert Hodges. These men were instructed to ignite the fuses, and to cast the grenades into forts, trenches, or amidst the ranks of their enemies, where the explosion was calculated to produce much execution; and the men, deriving their designation from the combustibles with which they were armed, were styled Grenadiers. Their duties were considered more arduous than those of the pikemen or musketeers; and the strongest and most active men were selected for the grenadier company. And although the hand-grenades have long been laid aside, yet one company, which is designated the "Grenadier Company," continues to form part of every battalion.

In 1679, Dumbarton's Regiment, which consisted at this period of twenty-one companies, was stationed in Ireland. In the autumn of this year, Tangier, in Africa (which had been ceded by Portugal to Charles II., in 1662, as part of the marriage-portion of his consort, Donna Catherina, Infanta of Portugal), was besieged by the Moors, who destroyed two forts at a short distance from the town, and then retired.

They, however, again appeared before the town in the spring of 1680, when four companies of Dumbarton's Regiment were ordered to reinforce the garrison; and these companies having embarked at Kinsale in the *James* and *Swan* frigates, landed at Tangier on the 4th of April.

Fort Henrietta, which stood at a short distance from the town, was at this time besieged by the Moors, and two breaches having been made, and the works undermined, the garrison could not maintain the place; consequently a sally from the city was resolved upon, to give the garrison an opportunity of blowing up the fort, and of cutting their passage through the Moorish Army to the town; and Captain Hume, Lieutenant Pierson, Lieutenant Bayley, four sergeants, and 80 private men, of Dumbarton's Regiment, were selected to form the forlorn-hope in the sally. Accordingly, at eight o'clock on the morning of the 12th of May, Dumbarton's veterans issued from the town, and made a gallant attack on the Moorish Army; at the same time the garrison in the fort blew up the building, and rushed forward, sword in hand, to cut their passage through the barbarians.

The conflict was sharp: the Moors came running forward in crowds to cut off this devoted band; yet these resolute Britons forced the first trench, and gained the second. This was, however, twelve feet deep; and while struggling to overcome the difficulty. Captain Trelawny and 120 men were killed by the Moors; and only forty-four officers and men succeeded in joining Captain Hume and his party of veteran Scots. This party was also attacked by several bodies of Moorish horsemen, who were all expert lancers; but the barbarians were repulsed. One Moorish chieftain rode over Captain Hume; but his horse fell, and the barbarian was immediately killed. The men continued skirmishing, and retiring in good order until they arrived under the protection of the guns of the fortress. The companies of Dumbarton's Regiment lost on this occasion fifteen men killed, and Captain Hume[1] and several men wounded.

In a few days after this action a cessation of hostilities was agreed upon with the Moors for four months; and during the summer twelve additional companies of Dumbarton's Regiment arrived at Tangier, from Ireland, under the command of Major Sir James Hackett. The arrival of these celebrated veterans is thus announced in one of the publications of that period:—

After this landed the valorous Major Hackett with the renowned regiment of the Earl of Dumbarton; all of them men of approved

---

1. "Captain Hume, who commanded our advance-party, showed great conduct and courage, standing several charges of the enemy's horse; and when the action was over, and he was upon his retreat to the main body, one of the Moors' chief commanders charged the rear of his party and overthrew him; but the Moor's horse falling, he was immediately killed."—*London Gazette*.

valour, fame having echoed the sound of their glorious actions and achievements in France and other nations; having left behind them a report of their glorious victories wherever they came; every place witnessing and giving large testimony of their renown: so that the arrival of this illustrious regiment more and more increased the resolutions and united the courage of the inhabitants, and added confidence to their valour.[2]

Hostilities again commenced in September, when the 1680 garrison quitted the town, and encamped under the walls; and the Lieut.-Governor, Sir Palmes Fairborne, is reported to have made the following speech to Dumbarton's Scots:—

> Countrymen and fellow-soldiers, let not your approved valour and fame in foreign nations be derogated at this time, neither degenerate from your ancient and former glory abroad; and as you are looked upon here to be brave and experienced soldiers (constant and successive victories having attended your conquering swords hitherto), do not come short of the great hopes we have in you, and the propitious procedures we expect from you at this time. For the glory of your nation, if you cannot surpass, you may imitate the bravest, and be emulous of their praises and renown.[3]

The expectations of the lieutenant-governor, with regard to these celebrated Scots, appear to have been realised; and in the various skirmishes and actions which followed, they always signalised themselves. In the account of a sharp action fought on the 20th of September, it is reported that;

> The grenadiers under Captain Hodges behaved themselves very bravely,

On the 22nd of the same month:

> Some of the Moorish horse advanced resolutely to the very line where our men were lodged, but were repulsed, and several of them killed. Several of the Scots grenadiers, who were very active and daring, advancing a little too far were killed, and others, advancing to their relief, were likewise hard put to it.

A sharp skirmish was afterwards kept up throughout the day, and:

---

2. *Tangier's Rescue* by John Ross, fol. 1681.
3. *Ibid.*

The Scots and the seamen from the fleet were hotly engaged, having beat the Moors out of several trenches.

While retiring, Captain Fitzpatrick was attacked by a Moorish chieftain, but was delivered by a shot which brought the barbarian down at the moment he was about to spear the captain. A Scots grenadier, of undaunted bravery, being desirous of possessing the Moor's charger, leaped over the trenches and seized the horse; but this brave man was immediately afterwards cut to pieces by a party of Moors, who came galloping forward at the moment he was about to retire with the horse. On the same day it was resolved, in consequence of a newly-erected fort being completed, to retire within the walls, when Sir James Hackett, at the head of Dumbarton's Scots, covered the retrograde movement, and repulsed several charges made by the Moorish lancers.

A sally was made from the town on the 24th of September, when the Scots again distinguished themselves, and had Captain Forbes and eight men killed. The lieut.-governor, Sir Palmes Fairborne, also received a mortal wound, and was succeeded in the command of the garrison by Lieut.-Colonel Sackville of the Foot Guards. On the 27th of September, a general sally of the garrison was made on the Moorish lines, where between fourteen and fifteen thousand barbarians were encamped. About three in the morning, the troops issued in silence from the town, and formed in order of battle. Soon afterwards the signal for the attack was given, when Dumbarton's[4] company of Scots grenadiers, led by Captain Hodges, and followed by the remaining companies of the regiment, rushed towards the Moorish lines with the velocity of lightning.

The Moors, who were reposing beyond their trenches, were suddenly aroused by the sound of a trampling multitude rushing to battle; and the next moment a shower of hand-grenades bursting amongst them put them in some confusion; yet they sprang to their arms, and, standing firm to receive the charge, disputed the ground with firmness. Soon the action became general, and:

> Nothing was heard but the roaring of cannon, the firing of muskets, and the loud acclamations of the Christians, who, ever and *anon*, when they gained any trench of the enemy, raised a shout which pierced the clouds, and echoed in the sky.[5]

---

4. "This day the Scots and their grenadiers charged first, if there was any time at all between their charging: for, like fire and lightning, all went on at once"—*Tangier's Rescue*.

5. *Ibid.*

Dumbarton's veterans quickly carried the first trench, then mixing in fierce combat with the Moors, soon proved that a valiant Scot was more than a match for one of the dusky sons of Africa. The first trench having been won, a portion of it was levelled for the cavalry, and the British and Spanish horsemen charged the Moors, and plunging amidst the dark masses, trampled and cut down the astonished Africans. At the same time the British grenadiers were seen using their hatchets with dreadful execution on one side, the pikemen were bearing down all before them on another, and, the musketeers, having slung their muskets, were fighting, sword in hand, with an impetuosity which the Moors could not withstand.

The waving masses of barbarians were broken, and they fled like a scattered swarm over the land; the British troops pursued, and a number of single combats followed, for the Moors were more expert in personal conflicts than in fighting in large bodies. These combats, however, generally terminated in favour of the British; and the Scots, particularly Captain Hodges and his grenadier company, were distinguished for the number they slew. Thus the siege of Tangier was raised, and Dumbarton's veteran Scots captured a splendid colour[6] from the Moors, The regiment lost [7] in this action, Lieutenants Scott and St. Leger; Ensigns Farrell, Murray, Bell, and Rhue; six sergeants, and thirty private soldiers killed; Captains Lockart, Lundy, Hume, Douglas, and

---

6. Four colours were captured in this action; one by Dumbarton's Scots, one by the admiral's battalion, one by the English horse, and one by the Spaniards. Three guns were also taken; two by the Foot Guards, and one by the battalion of Marines and Seamen.

7. The following return shows the loss sustained by the British troops in this engagement:—

Corps.	Killed.			Wounded.		
	Officers.	Men.	Horses.	Officers.	Men.	Horses.
Four troops of English Horse, now Royal Dragoons . . .	..	..	5	2	5	9
Three do. of Spanish Horse, disbanded in 1683	1	13	24	6	30	25
Battalion of Foot Guards . .	..	7	..	1	61	..
The Earl of Dumbarton's Regiment, now 1st Royal	6	36	..	15	100	..
The Earl of Inchiquin's do., now 2nd or Queen's Royal . .	2	34	..	10	124	..
Vice Admiral Herbert's Battalion, consisting of Marines and Seamen .	2	10	..	..	24	..
Total .	11	100	29	34	334	34

Narrative of the Siege of Tangier, published by authority, fol. 1680.

Percy; Lieutenants Glascock, Murray, Ennis, Corson, Bainesman, Macrohen, Stuart, Aukmooty, and Butler; with Ensign Mowast, and one hundred sergeants and private men wounded.

In a few days after this engagement a truce was concluded with the Moors for six months; and in the early part of December a regiment of foot (now the Fourth, or King's own), with 200 recruits for Dumbarton's Regiment, arrived from England.

During the winter, Lieut.-Colonel Kirk was sent on an embassy to Muley-Ismael, Emperor of Morocco. In the spring of 1681, a treaty of peace for four years was concluded and sent to England by Captain Thomas Langston.

King Charles II., however, (1682), found the maintenance of a sufficient garrison at Tangier too expensive to be continued without the aid of a grant from parliament. At the same time the nation was more alarmed at the prospect of a popish successor to the throne than at the apprehension of losing this fortress, which they feared would become a nursery for popish soldiers. The advantage derived from the Levant trade, and other arguments, were brought forward in favour of maintaining Tangier; but the parliament refused the necessary supply; and towards the end of 1683, Admiral Lord Dartmouth was jess sent with a fleet to demolish the fortress, and to bring away the garrison and British inhabitants.

One company of Dumbarton's Regiment arrived from Tangier, in November, 1683, and landed at Gravesend; and the remainder arrived in the river Thames in February, 1684, and, having landed at Rochester, were quartered—eight companies at Rochester and Chatham, six at Winchester, and two at Southampton. At the same time directions were sent to the Duke of Ormond, the Lord-Lieutenant of Ireland, to send the five companies of the regiment in that country to England.

In June of this year four companies attended the Duchess of York (afterwards Queen of England) at Tunbridge Wells; and in the autumn King Charles II. conferred upon this celebrated regiment the title of The Royal Regiment of Foot.[8]

---

8. The First Regiment of Foot Guards was for several years designated the *Royal Regiment*. There was also at this period a *Royal Regiment in Ireland*, which was sometimes styled Foot Guards. This corps adhered to King James II. at the Revolution in 1688. One battalion had previously arrived in England, and, being composed of papists, it was disbanded by William III. The men were confined a short time in the Isle of Wight, and afterwards transferred to the service of the Emperor of Germany. The other battalion fought in the cause of James II. in Ireland, until the surrender of Limerick in 1691, when it proceeded to France, and remained in the French service until it was disbanded.

On the 1st of October, sixteen companies of the Royal Regiment, commanded by Lieut.-Colonel Sir James Hackett, were reviewed, with a number of other corps, by King Charles II., on Putney Heath.

The Coldstream, my Lord Dumbarton's, and the Admiral's Battalions, successively exercised all three by beat of drum, the military postures of pike, sword, and musket, every man dexterously discharging his duties with an exact and general readiness, to the great delight of their Majesties and Royal Highnesses, who vouchsafed, all the time of exercise, to grace the arms with their presence. The other two battalions of the Royal Regiment [9] had not fallen short of the like performance, if illness of weather, when they just intended it, had not prevented: the day proving wet and showery was a general impediment from proceeding at that time to any other motions customary upon the like reviews; and all decamped Sooner than otherwise they would have done.

In the *Army List*, published by Nathan Brooks, in October, 1684, the Royal, or Dumbarton's Regiment, is stated to:

Consist of twenty-one companies, two lieutenants to each company, three sergeants, three corporals, and two drums, established; distinguished by red coats lined with white; sashes white, with a white fringe; breeches and stockings light grey; grenadiers distinguished by caps lined white, the lion's face, proper, crowned; flys St. Andrew's cross, with thistle and crown, circumscribed in the centre, *Nemo me impunè lacessit.*

After the review, the regiment was stationed in extensive cantonments in the county of Kent, where it remained until the death of King Charles II., on the 6th February, 1685, when it was suddenly ordered to march into quarters in London and the adjacent villages.[10] Although King James II. was known to be a papist, yet no opposition was made to his accession to the throne; and in March four companies proceeded to Yarmouth, and four to Rochester, leaving thirteen companies in quarters in the metropolis.

---

9. The author of the account of this review here means two battalions of the 1st Foot Guards.
10. War Office Records.

REVIEWING THE COLDSTREAMERS

Story of the Royal Scots

By Lawrence Weaver

The year 1677 marked a turning-point in the policy of England, too long a cat's-paw of Louis XIV. Charles II, much as he had relied on the secret pension from the French king, was driven by national feeling to range himself with the Dutch against Louis' pretensions. The British troops were recalled, and on January 29, 1678, Lord Dumbarton went to France "to bring away his regiment." Louis raised a punctilio about their departure, and the first companies 1678 seem not to have reached England until March 11, or the last until September, on the first of which month they mustered in Hertfordshire, twenty-one companies strong. Incorporated in Dumbarton's regiment—as it was now called—were the remains of another Scots regiment which had been raised for the French service by Lord James Douglas,[1] brother of Lord Dumbarton.

It is, as Pepys would say, pretty to see how the old regiment went on from strength to strength, absorbing weaker elements continually, and always strengthening its own personality in the process.

This year of return was also marked by a change in organisation and equipment. A company of grenadiers was added under the command of Captain Robert Hodges. As John Evelyn said with truth, this was "a new kind of soldier," begotten by new methods of warfare and the increasing use of field fortifications. They were strong picked men armed like other musketeers, with the addition of a pouch suspended from a broad buff belt which passed over the left shoulder, and containing three hand grenades.

The ordinary broad-brimmed hat of the period was replaced (in the Grenadier company) by the high conical cap, which looks so im-

---

1. Not to be confounded with the Lord James, who was colonel from 1637 to 1645. They were half-brothers.

posing in old pictures. Its practical merit was that it enabled the musket to be unslung rather more readily, but its aesthetic merit no doubt counted a good deal in days when the pomp and circumstance of war gave abiding pleasure. Even so, its height must have made undue difficulty in unslinging the musket, for it gave way not long after to a cloth cap.

Nathan Brooks' *Army List* of 1684 says that the regiment was:

Distinguished by red coats lined with white; sashes white, with a white fringe; breeches and stockings light grey; grenadiers distinguished by caps lined white, the lion's face proper crowned. (etc.)

PRIVATE IN GRENADIER COMPANY, 1684.

It is worth noting that our regiments in the trenches in France have lately renewed the grenadier tradition by the use of hand-thrown bombs to an extent not previously known in modern warfare (1914-1918). In 1679 the regiment was transferred to the Irish establishment and landed at Kinsale in April. It then consisted, when at full strength, of twenty-one companies, each including three sergeants, three corporals, two drummers, and fifty privates. There were eighty-two officers, excluding the staff officers, *i. e.* adjutant, chaplain, chirurgeon and his mate, quarter-master, 1679 drum major and piper major. The colonel was a Roman Catholic, and his commission was therefore in abeyance; meanwhile he was appointed to the command in Scotland.

Nothing interesting happened in Ireland, and in 1680 the siege of Tangier by the Moors led to sixteen companies being shipped thither. Those who sailed in H.M.S. *Phoenix* were pursued by a "Turk's mann of war of about 22 or 24 gunnes," but a shot from the *Ruby* and the sight of the English ensign caused her to haul off. Tangier had been a troublesome possession since it came to the English crown as part of the dowry of Charles the Second's Portuguese consort, as readers of Pepys' *Diary* well know. The Moors were not only brave but scientific soldiers, and their siege works were skilfully contrived. Eighty-four of the veteran Scots made a brilliant sally on May 12 to rescue the garrison of an outlying fort which was to be blown up. The Moorish Army lay between. The men from the fort lost a captain and one hundred and twenty men, and only forty-four succeeded in joining the rescuing Scots, who themselves lost fifteen killed, and their gallant leader, Captain Hume, was wounded.

After four months' peace the struggle began again in September, when the grenadier company in particular behaved themselves "very bravely." Their hatchets were pretty weapons in a hand-to-hand fight. Major Hackett was then in command of the regiment, and the struggle continued with little intermission until October 27,[2] when a general sally against the Moorish lines was crowned with success. It was a desperate business. The story is long and lively, but it has been told by Colonel Davis [3] and retold in the *Records*, so it need not be repeated here. Dumbarton's bore the brunt of the fighting, and the casualties were very heavy.

The Moors were glad to make terms, and peace continued until the British ended their occupation of Tangier in 1683. Meanwhile the

---

2. Not of September, as Cannon says.
3. In his *History of the Second Foot.*

king had no quarrel for his faithful Scots to prosecute, so they enlivened the weariness of garrison duty by private bickerings. There were duels between officers and bloody fracas between men: also questions of precedence between the governor and the officers of Dumbarton's, which led to lively argument.

After the demolition of the Mole, the forts and the town, a long and laborious business, the garrison sailed for England, Dumbarton's crowned with glory gained by fighting under new conditions in a new continent. The regiment reached England in the winter of 1683–1684, and the five companies which had remained in Ireland since 1680 came over to join the sixteen from foreign service.

In 1678 the regiment was in some danger of disbandment. In the Proceedings of the House of Lords, December 16, 1678, upon a Bill for disbanding some of the Forces, there appears in the list the Regiment of Foot of George, Earl of Dumbarton. [4] Happily the Lords did not use the besom of destruction.

---

4. *Clifford Walton*, note.

Historical Record 1st or Royal Dragoons

By General de Ainslie

In the year 1664, King Charles II. having contracted an alliance with Donna Catherina, Infanta of Portugal, and receiving as her marriage portion a sum of money equal to £300,000, together with the island of Bombay in the East Indies and the city of Tangiers in Africa, this last acquisition, with its important fortress, its harbour and local advantages, appeared to open out a new field for commercial enterprise, to be followed, it was expected, by the acquirement of extensive possessions in that country, and in consequence a garrison of four regiments of Foot and a troop of Horse was appointed to that place, of which the Earl of Peterborough was constituted Captain-General, Chief Governor, and Admiral.

Three of the regiments of Foot, commanded respectively by Sir Robert Harley and Colonels Fitzgerald and O'Farell, were taken from the garrison of Dunkirk; the other regiment, now the 2nd or Queen's Royal, and the troop of Horse, the nucleus, as will be subsequently seen, of the Royal Regiment of Dragoons, had been raised in England by the Earl of Peterborough in the autumn of 1661, and were mustered, the former on Putney Heath, and the latter in St. George's Fields, Southwark, in October that year.

The troop of Horse consisted of three officers, one quartermaster, four corporals, and 100 privates; the ranks were completed with veterans of the Civil War, who were armed with *cuirasses*, iron headpieces called potts, long swords, and a pair of large pistols to which a short carbine was afterwards added. They were mounted upon long-tailed horses of superior weight and power; wore high boots reaching to the middle of the thigh, and scarlet vests. The officers wore hats decorated

Uniform of 1660

with a profusion of feathers, and both officers and men ornamented their horses' heads and tads with large bunches of ribbons.

The officers of this troop were the Earl of Peterborough, Captain and Colonel; Robert Leech, Captain-Lieutenant; James Mordaunt, Cornet.

The appearance and equipment of the officers and men were much commended in the publications of that period. They embarked in the middle of December, 1661; and in a letter to the Earl of Peterborough, dated the 20th of the month, the king observes:—

I desire you to lett those honest men knowe who are along with you yet they shall allways be in my particular care and protection as persons yet venture themaelvea in my service; and so, wishing you a good voyage,

I remain, &c.,

Charles R.

The troops arrived at Tangiers in January, 1662, and war commencing soon afterwards between the British in this part of Africa and the Moors, frequent encounters took place between the garrison and the barbarians, to the decided advantage of the former, and in which the English horsemen became celebrated for gallant conduct.

In 1663 the veteran Earl of Teviot, who had been appointed Governor of Tangiers in succession to the Earl of Peterborough, occasionally penetrated into the adjacent country at the head of a party of Horse, who performed many brilliant exploits on the neighbouring plains and among the rocks and woods, where they frequently surprised lurking bodies of the Moors and made captures of cattle and other spoil. These Africans, however, were clever horsemen, and fought with lances, swords, and short fusils.

In February, 1664, a Moorish army, commanded by Gaylan the usurper of Fez, appeared before Tangiers with the object of laying siege to the fortress. On the 1st of March the Earl of Teviot observing a body of the enemy, with a splendid scarlet standard, on an eminence near the city, ordered the troop of Horse to make a sally and bring in the standard, which command being promptly obeyed, the brave troopers, led by Captain Witham, issued from the city, traversed the intervening space with signal intrepidity, and, having routed the Moors, they returned in triumph with the standard, which they hoisted ou one of the towers of the fortress, to the surprise and chagrin of the Moorish chiefs, who from a distance with the main body of their army had witnessed this feat of arms.

On the 13th of March the *cuirassiers* had a smart affair with some of the enemy's best cavalry; and on the 27th the Earl of Teviot in person led them against a horde of Lancers and Foot, who were hiding in ambush, when the barbarians were routed and pursued among the rocks and broken ground with great slaughter. On the 4th of May, however, the English met with a severe repulse, when the governor, deceived by a false report, advanced too far into the interior, and, being surprised by a numerous band of Moors, a fearful massacre ensued, and the gallant Earl of Teviot was numbered among the slain.

Frequent affairs happened during the subsequent years between the English and the Moors, in which desultory warfare the troop of Horse continued to maintain its high character. Hostilities were occasionally suspended and renewed after short intervals of peace, and during seventeen years the garrison of Tangiers resisted with success every attempt made upon the city.

In 1679 a numerous army appeared before Tangiers, and destroyed the forts constructed at a distance from the city, after which they withdrew, but reappeared in the spring of 1680, in increased numbers and with swarms of clever horsemen on light and swift horses, who, hovering round the walls, confined the Christians within narrow limits. King Charles II. despatched a battalion of the Foot Guards and sixteen companies of Dumbartons, now the 1st or Royal Scots Regiment, to reinforce the garrison, and issued commissions for raising in England a regiment of Foot, now the 4th or King's Own, and six troops of Horse, while at the same time arrangements were made for procuring the services of three troops of Spanish Cavalry.

The six troops of English Horse were raised respectively by Major-General the Earl of Ossory; Colonel Sir John Lanier; Captains Robert Pulteney, John Coy, Charles Nedby, and Thomas Langston. The three last-named officers having been Captains in the Duke of Monmouth's regiment of Horse—which had been disbanded only a few months before—their troops were speedily completed with disciplined soldiers who also had served in that regiment, and the demand for Cavalry at Tangiers being urgent they were at once supplied with horses and equipment from the Life Guards, and arrived at Tangiers in the early part of September, 1680, at the same time as the three troops of Spanish Cavalry arrived there from Gibraltar.

The cavalry at Tangiers now consisted of seven troops of efficient *cuirassiers*, who were engaged on the 12th of September, when the

Moorish Horse were driven from under the walls and several out-works of the fortifications were recovered. Another sally was on the 20th, and on the following day the *cuirassier's* had a smart skirmish with the Moorish lancers and had eight men killed and twenty wounded. An attack on the enemy's lines was made on the 24th, when the governor, Sir Palmes Fairborne, was mortally wounded.

On the 27th of September the garrison, amounting to about 4,000 men, issued from the fortress and attacked the army of the Moors, estimated at 18,000 men, in their entrenched camp with signal audacity. So eager was the cavalry to engage that a dispute actually arose between the English and Spanish Horse, each claiming the honour of making the first charge, when the matter being referred to the Lieutenant Governor, Colonel Sackville, he gave the Spaniards the precedence because they fought as "auxiliaries." The Moors having a great superiority of numbers stood their ground for some time with much resolution, and the thunder of artillery, the roll of musketry, the clash of arms, the loud shouts of the British and the wild cries of the Africans produced an awful scene of carnage and confusion.

The English and Spanish Horse stood in column of troops until the first entrenchment was carried and a apace levelled for the passage of the cavalry, when they dashed through the opening and rushed at full speed upon the dark masses of the defenders, who were broken, trampled down, and pursued with dreadful slaughter, while the musketeers, pikemen and grenadiers followed with loud shouts as the dismayed Africans fell beneath the sabres of the English and Spanish troopers. Many of the Moors faced about and confronted their pursuers; numerous single combats took place, and the vicinity of the camp was covered with slain. Captain Nedby's troop of English Horse particularly distinguished itself, and captured a standard of curious workmanship. The Spaniards also captured a colour, Dumbarton's "Scots" another, and a fourth was taken by a battalion of marines and seamen from the fleet.

The Moorish legions having been driven from before the city with severe loss, this victory was followed by a treaty of peace, when the troops of Horse raised by the Earl of Ossory, Sir John Lanier, and Captain Pulteney, not having left England were disbanded.

The improved military system introduced among the Moors by European renegades rendering it now necessary to employ at Tangiers a much stronger garrison than hitherto, the question was brought before Parliament, but no grant of money being voted, it was decided by the Government to destroy the works and withdraw the troops.

At this period the attention of King Charles II. was particularly directed to the improvement of his army, and resolving to retain the services of the Tangiers Horse, His Majesty commissioned Colonel John Churchill to raise a troop of dragoons at St. Albans and its vicinity; and Viscount Cornbury, son of the Earl of Clarendon, to raise another at Hertford; and His Majesty constituted these two, with the four troops of Tangiers Horse, a regiment to which he gave the distinguished title of "The King's Own Royal Regiment of Dragoons"; the words "King's Own" were, however, soon afterwards discontinued, and the regiment was styled "The Royal Regiment of Dragoons." In 1672 a corps had been raised bearing this title, but it was disbanded after the Peace of Nimeguen in October of that year. The Colonelcy of the new regiment was conferred upon Colonel Churchill, now advanced to the dignity of Baron Churchill of Eyemouth, by commission, dated 19th of November, 1683, and the Lieut.-Colonelcy at the same time upon Viscount Cornbury.

> Charles R.
>
> Our will and pleasure is that as soon as the troop of our Royal Regiment of Dragoons, whereof Charles Nedby, Esq., is captain, shall arrive from our garrisons at Tangiers, you cause the same forthwith to march to the town of Ware, in our county of Hertford, where they are to remain until further orders; and the officers of the said troops are to take care that the soldiers duly pay their intended quarters.
>
> Given at our Court at Whitehall, this 18th day of February, 1623.
>
> > By His Majesty's command,
> >
> > > William Blathwayte.

A similar order was given for Captain Thomas Langston's troop to quarter at Hoddesdon, Captain John Coy's at Hampstead, and Captain Alexander Mackenzie's (the troops raised in 1661) at Watford and Bushey.—*War Office Records.*

The establishment was fixed, by a warrant bearing date the 18th of January, 1684, from which the following is an extract:—

> Charles R.
>
> Charles the Second, by the Grace of God King of England, Scotland, France and Ireland, Defender of the Faith, &c.

Our will and pleasure is that this establishment of our Guards, Cuirassiers, and land forces within our Kingdom of England, Dominion of Wales, and Town of Berwick-upon-Tweed and the Islands thereunto belonging, and of all other offices and charges therein expressed, do commence on the 1st day of January, 1683—4, in the thirty-fifthe year of our reign.

His Majesty's own Royal Regiment of Dragoons,—*10th page, Records C.*

HIS MAJESTY'S OWN ROYAL REGIMENT OF DRAGOONS.			
STAFF OFFICERS.	Per Diem.		
	£	s.	d.
Colonel, *as Colonel*, xii*, and iij horses iij*	0	15	0
Lieutenant-Colonel, *as Lieut.-Colonel*, vij*, and ij horses ij*	0	9	0
Major, as Major v*, and j horse j*	0	6	0
Chaplaine	0	6	8
Chirurgeon iv*, and j horse to carry his chest, ij* . .	0	6	0
Adjutant iv*, and for his horse j*	0	5	0
Quarter-Master and Marshal in one person iv*, his horse j*	0	5	0
Gunsmith iv*, and his servant i*	0	5	0
	2	17	8
THE COLONEL'S TROOP.			
The Colonel, *as Captaine*, viii*, and iij horses iij* . .	0	11	0
Lieutenant iv*, and ij horses ij*	0	6	0
Cornett iij*, and ij horses ij*	0	5	0
Quarter-Master, for himself and horse	0	4	0
Two Serjeants each j* vi⁴, and ij* for horses	0	5	0
Three Corporals each j*, and iij* for horses	0	6	0
Two Drummers each j*, and ij* for horses	0	4	0
Two Hautboys each i*, and ij* for horses	0	4	0
Fifty Soldiers each i* vi⁴ for man and horse	3	15	0
	6	0	0
Five Troops more at the same rate	30	0	0
The Major to have no Troop, but instead thereof the pay of a Captain xi*, in lieu of servants iii* . . .	0	14	0
TOTAL . .	39	11	8
TOTAL PER ANNUM . . . . £14,447 18s. 4d.			

The four troops from Tangiers arrived in England in February, 1684, and having returned their *cuirasses* into store, the whole were equipped as dragoons, and the following arms and appointments were issued to the regiment from the Tower of London, *viz.*,

316 Muskets and bayonets.

12 Halberds.

12 Partisans.

12 Drums.

316 Cartouch boxes and belts.

318 Waist belts and bayonet frogs.

358 Saddles and bridles.

388 Sets of holster caps and housings.

—War Office Records.

The uniform of the regiment was scarlet lined with blue. The men wore hats bound with silver lace, and ornamented with ribbons, having a metal head-piece fastened inside the crown; also high boots. Their horse furniture was of scarlet cloth trimmed with blue, with the king's cipher embroidered in yellow on the housings and holster caps.

The drummers and hautboys were clothed in splendid uniforms, which, according to the *War Office Records*, cost upwards of £10 per suit, and each troop was furnished with a crimson standard or guidon, having the following devices embroidered thereon, *viz.*;—

On the standard of the colonel's troop: the king's cipher and crown; the lieutenant-colonel's troop the rays of the sun, proper, crowned, issuing out of a cloud, proper—a badge used by the Black Prince.

The first troop: the top of a beacon crowned, or, with flames of fire, proper—a badge of Henry V.

The second troop: three ostrich feathers, crowned, argent—a badge of Henry VI.

The third troop: a rose and pomegranate impaled, leaves and stalk vert—a badge of Henry VII.

The fourth troop: a phoenix in flames, proper—a badge of Queen Elizabeth.[1]

The following officers were at this period holding commissions in the regiment:—

---

1. Nathan Brook's *Complete List Military*. London, 1684.

TROOPS.	CAPTAINS.	LIEUTENANTS.	CORNETS
Colonels . .	Lord Churchill.	Thos. Hussey.	Wm. Hussey.
Lieut.-Cols. .	Visc. Cornbury.	Charles Ward.	Piercy Roche.
1st Troop . .	Alex. Mackenzie.	H. Wyndham.	John Cole.
2nd "	Chas. Nedby.	John Williams.	George Clifford.
3rd "	John Coy.	Charles La Rue.	William Stamford.
4th "	Thomas Langston.	F. Langston.	Thomas Pownel.

Hugh Sutherland . . . . . . Major.
Thomas Crawley . . . . . . Adjutant.
Henry Hawker . . . . Quarter-Master and Marshal.
Theobald Churchill . . . . . Chaplain.
Peregrine Yewel . . . . . . Chirurgeon.

Lieutenant Hugh Wyndham became afterwards colonel of the 7th Horse, the present 6th Dragoon Guards, the Carbineers.

Lieutenant Francis Langston was subsequently colonel of the 5th Horse, 4th R. I. Dragoon Guards.

1. The Watergate or Sandwich Tower.
2. English Church. 3. Portuguese Church.

Part of Tangier from above, 1.

The Left Ballivy

without the Water-gate,   4 The Head Court of Guard.

W. Hollar delineavit et sculpsit 16..

The First or the Royal Regiment of Dragoons

Richard Cannon

The anarchy, devastation, and bloodshed which 1661 had prevailed in Britain during the rebellion and tyrannical usurpation of Cromwell, having been succeeded by the restoration of monarchy,—the despotic sway of sectarians and republicans put down by the establishment of a regular government on constitutional principles,—and the army of the commonwealth disbanded, King Charles II. directed his attention to domestic concerns, and engaged in a matrimonial alliance with Donna Catherina, Infanta of Portugal; and this event gave rise to the formation of a troop of *cuirassiers*, which was the nucleus of the corps now bearing the distinguished title of The Royal Regiment of Dragoons.

By the marriage treaty the ancient and once magnificent city of Tangier, in Africa, and the island of Bombay in the East Indies, were ceded by the king of Portugal to the British crown; and, with a sum equal to three hundred thousand pounds, constituted the *infanta's* dowry.

As the possession of the important fortress of Tangier, with its harbour and local advantages, appeared to open a new field for commercial pursuits, and was expected to be followed by the acquisition of extensive possessions in that part of the world, four regiments of foot and a troop of horse were appointed to garrison that fortress, and the Earl of Peterborough was constituted captain general, chief governor, and vice admiral of that part of His Majesty's dominions.

Three of the regiments of foot, commanded by Sir Robert Harley, and Colonels Fitzgerald and O'Farell, were withdrawn from the garrison of Dunkirk, and were composed of men who had fought in the royal cause during the civil war, and afterwards in the Netherlands. The other regiment of foot, (now the second, or Queen's royal,) and the troop of Horse (now Royal Dragoons) were raised in England by the Earl of Peterborough in the autumn of 1661, and were mustered, the former on Putney Heath, and the latter in St. George's Fields, Southwark, in October.[1]

The troop of Horse consisted of three officers, one quartermaster, four corporals, one trumpeter, and one hundred private men; the ranks were completed with veterans of the civil war, who were armed with *cuirasses*, iron head-pieces called potts, long swords, and a pair of large pistols, to which a short carbine was afterwards added: they were mounted on long-tailed horses of superior 1661 weight and power, wore high boots reaching to the middle of the thigh, and scarlet vests: the officers wore hats decorated with a profusion of feathers; and both officers and men ornamented their horses' heads and tails with large bunches of ribands. The officers of this troop were,

The Earl of Peterborough, Captain and Colonel.

Robert Leech, Captain-Lieutenant.

James Mordaunt, Cornet.

The appearance and equipment of the officers and men were commended in the ephemeral publications of that period. They embarked in the middle of December, and in a letter to the Earl of Peterborough, dated the 21st of December, the king observed:—

I desire you to lett those honest men knowe who are along with you, yet they shall allwayes be in my particular care and protection as persons yet venture themselves in my service. And so, wishing you a good voyage,

I remain, &c.,

Charles R.[2]

The troops arrived at Tangier in January, 1662 and a war commencing soon afterwards between the British occupants of this part of Africa and the Moors, frequent encounters occurred between detachments of the garrison of Tangier and the barbarians, in which the former had a decided superiority, and the English horsemen became celebrated for gallant achievements.[3]

1. *Bibl. Harl.* No. 1595.—*Mercurius Publicus.*—*Kingdom's Intelligencer.*—*War-Office Records.*—*History of Tangier,* &c.
2. *Bibl. Harl.* 6844.
3. *History of Tangier,* 8vo., 1664

CAPTURE OF MOORISH STANDARD BY THE ENGLISH HORSE AT TANGIERS IN 1664.
NOW 1ST DRAGOONS.

The veteran Earl of Teviot, who was appointed governor of Tangier in 1663, in succession to the Earl of Peterborough, occasionally penetrated into the adjacent country at the head of a detachment of horse, and many brilliant exploits were performed by the gallant English troopers, among the rocks, in the woods, and on the plains of this part of Africa, where they frequently surprised lurking parties of Moors, and captured cattle and other booty. The Africans were, however, expert horsemen, and fought with lance, sword, and short fusils.

In February, 1664, a Moorish army, commanded by Gaylan, usurper of Fez, appeared before Tangier to besiege the fortress. On the 1st of March the Earl of Teviot, observing a body of Moors, with a splendid scarlet standard, stationed on an eminence near the city, ordered the troop of Horse to sally and bring in the standard. The command was instantly obeyed; the brave troopers, led by Captain Witham, issued from the city, traversed the intervening space with signal intrepidity, routed the Moorish band, and captured the standard, with which they returned in triumph to the fortress, and erected it on the top of one of the towers, to the surprise and chagrin of the Moorish chiefs, who, being posted at a distance with the main body of their army, witnessed this brilliant exploit.

On the 13th of March the English horsemen had a sharp encounter with some of the enemy's best cavalry; and on the 27th, the Earl of Teviot led them against a horde of Moorish lancers and foot who were concealed in ambush, and the barbarians were routed and pursued among the woods and broken grounds with great slaughter. The English horsemen, however, suffered severely on the 4th of May in the same year, when the governor, having been deceived by a false report, advanced too far into the country, and was surprised by a numerous band of Moors in ambush. A fearful slaughter followed, and the Earl of Teviot was numbered among the slain.

Frequent encounters took place in the subsequent years between detached parties of British and Moors, and in this desultory warfare the English horsemen preserved their high character. Hostilities were occasionally terminated, and renewed after short intervals of peace; and during the period of seventeen years the garrison resisted, with firmness and success, every attempt of the Moors against the city.

In 1679 a numerous army of Moors appeared before Tangier, and destroyed two forts situate at a distance from the town. They afterwards withdrew, but reappeared in the spring of 1680, with augmented numbers, and swarms of expert Moorish lancers, on light and swift horses, hovered round the fortress and confined the Christians within narrow limits. King Charles II. sent a battalion of foot guards and sixteen companies of Dumbarton's (now First Royal) regiment, to reinforce the garrison, and issued commissions for raising a regiment of foot (now the fourth, or the King's own) and six troops of Horse in England: at the same time arrangements were made for procuring the service of three troops of Spanish cavalry.

The six troops of English horse were raised by Major-General the Earl of Ossory, Lieutenant-Colonel Sir John Lanier,[5] Captains Robert Pulteney, John Coy,[6] Charles Nedby, and Thomas Langston:[7] the three last-named officers having been captains in the Duke of Monmouth's regiment of horse, which was disbanded only a few months before, their troops were speedily completed with disciplined men who had served in that regiment; and the demand for cavalry at Tangier being urgent, they were furnished with horses and equipment from the Life Guards, and arrived at Tangier in the early part of September: at the same time the three troops of Spanish horse arrived from Gibraltar.

The cavalry at Tangier now consisted of seven efficient troops of *cuirassiers*, who were engaged in a sally on the 12th of September, when the Moorish horsemen were driven from under the walls, and several outworks were recovered from the barbarians. Another sally was made on the 21st of the same month, and on the following day the English *cuirassiers* had a sharp skirmish with the Moorish lancers, and had eight men killed and twenty wounded. An attack was made on the 1680 enemy's lines on the 24th of September, when the governor, Sir Palmes Fairborne, was mortally wounded.

On the 27th of September, the garrison, amounting to about 4000 men, issued from the fortress and attacked the Moorish army of about 15,000 men in its entrenched camp with signal gallantry. So eager were the troopers to engage their adversaries that a dispute occurred between the English and Spanish horse, each claiming the honour of charging first: the subject was referred to the lieutenant-governor, Colonel Sackville, who gave the Spaniards the precedence on this oc-

---

4. Sir John Lanier was afterwards colonel of the Queen's Horse, now First Dragoon Guards. John Coy was afterwards colonel of the Seventh Horse, now Fifth Dragoon Guards.

5. Thomas Langston was celebrated for taking the Princess Anne of Denmark's regiment of horse over to the Prince of Orange at the Revolution in 1688: he was appointed colonel of that regiment on the 31st of December, 1688, and died in Ireland in 1689: the regiment was disbanded in 1692.

6. *Vide* the Historical Record of the Life Guards.

casion, because they fought as auxiliaries. The Moors, having a great superiority of numbers, stood their ground resolutely for some time; and the thunder of cannon, the roll of musketry, the clash of arms, the loud shouts of the British, the cries of the Africans, produced an awful scene of carnage and confusion.

The English horse stood in column of troops until the first entrenchment was carried, and a space levelled for the cavalry to pass, when they filed through the aperture and rushed at speed upon the dark masses of barbarians, who were broken, trampled down, and pursued with a dreadful slaughter; while the musketeers, pikemen, and grenadiers followed, shouting as the dismayed Africans fell in succession beneath the sabres of the English and Spanish troopers. Many of the Moors faced about and confronted their pursuers; numerous single combats took place, and the vicinity of the camp was covered with slain. Captain Nedby's troop of English horse particularly distinguished itself, and captured a splendid Moorish colour of curious workmanship. The Spaniards also captured a colour, Dumbarton's Scots another, and a fourth was taken by a battalion of marines and seamen from the fleet.[7]

The Moorish legions, having been driven from before the town with severe loss, this victory was followed by a treaty of peace, and the troops of horse raised by the Earl of Ossory, Sir John Lanier, and Robert Pulteney, not having left England, were disbanded.

The improved military system, introduced in 1862, among the Moors by European renegades, having rendered it necessary to employ a much stronger garrison at Tangier than formerly, the subject was brought before parliament, 1683, but the question of a popish successor to the throne was agitating the people, and no grant was voted. The king, being unwilling to bear the expense of the fortifications and troops without pecuniary aid from parliament, resolved to destroy the works and mole, and to withdraw the garrison.

---

7. Narrative of the great engagement at Tangier; *Tangier's Rescue*, by John Ross; *London Gazettes*, &c. &c.

York.
G

Monmouth

Cambridge

B

Pole

D

The
New
Haven

A

E

F

S. Moore Sc.

A. Whitehall   C. Irish battery   E. York Castle   G. Charles F.
B. Bridges   D. S.t Catharin   F. Upper Ca.   H. Henrieta

M

Lames

Great Valley

G

K

M

L

I Whitby   L. Fince Slain May 16. 1564
K. Moores T. M The Moores Ambassad of Horse

The Origin and History of First or Grenadier Guards

By F. W. Hamilton

The services of part of the King's Regiment of Foot Guards were in the month of June, 1680, called into requisition in another quarter of the world. Tangiers, which had become an appanage of the British Crown upon the marriage of Charles II. with Catherine, Princess of Portugal, in 1661, had been frequently exposed to the inroads of its neighbours, and its British garrison now required reinforcements to enable it to withstand the repeated attacks of the Moors. A succinct account of the history of this dependency from that time will show more clearly the necessity for sending out at this period additional troops for its defence.

When Tangiers, in 1661, first came under British rule, Lord Peterborough was transferred from the government of Dunkirk to be its governor, and though he took possession of his new government without much opposition, he shortly experienced great difficulties, arising from the jealousy of the Moors at their new neighbours. These Moors were in the constant habit of attacking any parties who, without sufficient escort, ventured into the country. Lord Rutherford, the successor of Lord Peterborough at Dunkirk in 1661, was, upon the sale of that town to the French in 1662, created Lord Teviot, and appointed, in 1663, to succeed Lord Peterborough in the government of Tangiers.

He arrived there on the 1st of May, bringing with him a reinforcement of 400 men of the late garrison of Dunkirk; he reorganised the troops, embodying all the Irish into one regiment, under Colonel Fitzgerald, and the English into another called the Governor's Regiment, now the 2nd regiment of the line, of which he himself was appointed colonel, and Henry Norwood its lieutenant-colonel. Lord Teviot at once proceeded to erect several forts outside the town, in order to give the garrison command of its immediate neighbourhood; he made a truce with Gayland, the Moorish chief, and on the 23rd of July articles of peace for a truce of six months were signed between the English and the Moors. At the expiration of that period, Lord Teviot continued his works of improvement, though constantly exposed to attacks from the Moors, till, on the 1st of May, 1664, when reconnoitring the ground in the neighbourhood, not properly supported by his cavalry, he was surprised and killed, with most of his party.

Colonel John Fitzgerald, colonel of the Irish regiment, was appointed governor in his place on the 7th of June, 1664.

Lord Bellasis succeeded Fitzgerald before March, 1665, and turned his attention to keeping the garrison in a state of efficiency and to endeavouring to make a treaty with the Moors. Having effected this in the spring of 1666, he left Colonel Norwood as lieutenant-governor during his absence, and returned to England. The garrison, under Colonel Norwood, consisting of the English and Irish regiments, 800 strong each, and of one troop of horse, besides 12 guns, continued to be well supplied with provisions by Taffaleta and Gayland, and during his tenure of office and that of his successor. Lord Middleton, who was appointed governor in 1670, the affairs of the garrison continued to be satisfactory.

But little change occurred during the next few years: at one time a temporary truce would exist between the English and the Moors; but it was frequently interrupted by sudden incursions on the part of the latter. In 1675, the Earl of Inchiquin succeeded as governor, a post which he retained for four years, when in February, 1679, Sir Palmes Fairburn succeeded him.

The year after Sir Palmes' arrival, the Alcade of Alcazar, Omar Ben Hadden, encouraged by former successes, and in hopes of finally driving the Christians out of the Moorish empire, advanced against Tangiers with an army of about 7000 men. He commenced the siege on the 25th of March, 1680, and prosecuted it with so much vigour, mining towards Charles Fort, that its detached garrison, 170 strong, was forced to abandon it on the 14th of May, leaving thirteen guns behind in the fort, and losing during its retreat its commanding officer, Captain Trelawny, and 126 men. Shortly afterwards Pole Fort, which covered the main gates of the town and the Norwood redoubt, were found untenable, and on the 19th of May, Sir Palmes Fairburn offered to treat with the Moors. This was accepted, and both parties agreed to a cessation of hostilities for four months.

A report of the state of affairs was at once sent to England, and the necessity of immediate succour being sent out, was represented to the home authorities, if the town was to remain a British possession. Under these circumstances, it was resolved to send out reinforcements without delay, and amongst other corps ordered to be formed for this service, was a combined battalion, 600 strong, to be divided into five companies of 120 men each, composed of drafts from the two regiments of Foot Guards and from some of the garrisons in England, in the following proportions:—

240 men from the First or King's Regiment of Foot Guards, in two companies, commanded respectively by Lieut.-Colonels Edward Sackville and Bowes.
120 men from the Coldstreams, in one company under Captain Tollemache.
100 men from the Portsmouth garrison.
80 men from the Plymouth garrison.
30 men from the three garrison companies in the Tower.
30 men from the companies in the Isle of Wight.

These last 240 men from various garrison companies were to be formed into two companies, under Captain Fawtrey and Captain Philip Kirk. The subalterns attached to Colonel Sackville's company were Lieutenant Francis Hawley, subsequently captain of a garrison company, and Lieutenant Church. Those to Captain Bowes's company were Lieutenant Robinson and Ensign Heron.

Each of the two companies of the King's Regiment of Foot Guards received, as usual, a colour, with one of the royal badges of the regiment emblazoned thereon. The command of this corps, which received the appellation of the "King's Battalion," was given to Lieutenant-Colonel Edward Sackville, an old and experienced officer, who had served in the King's Regiment of Foot Guards, but had retired in November, 1675. Sir Samuel Clarke, the lieutenant-colonel of the regiment, who had returned from service in the Low Countries in the previous year, had, in the first instance, been appointed by the king to act as major-general in command of all the troops at Tangiers; but upon Lieutenant-Colonel Edward Sackville being appointed to command the King's Battalion, June 2nd, 1680, the commission of Sir Samuel Clarke was revoked. The battalion was soon formed; and having embarked in the course of the month of on board transports in the Thames, was conveyed to its destination.

The garrison had been anxiously looking out for the reliefs from England, when, on the 2nd of July, the King's Battalion, composed, as we have seen, of a large proportion of Guardsmen, and consequently sometimes called the Guards Battalion, landed at Tangiers under Sackville. With them came some volunteers, who had been induced by the young Earl of Plymouth to join the expedition, with drafts of four independent companies; these were eventually attached to Lord Dumbarton's Scots regiment, when that corps, which had but recently returned from France, arrived in the colony under the command of Lieutenant-Colonel Halket.

The inhabitants, who, previous to the arrival of these two regiments, had been forced to a cessation of hostilities, were now anxious both to renew the war and to revenge themselves for all the injuries to which they had hitherto been forced to submit. Immediately upon landing, Colonels Sackville and Halket exerted themselves in perfecting the drill and discipline of their respective corps, which so much met with the approval of the lieutenant-governor, that he directed the Governor's Regiment to pursue the same system.

The expiration of the four months' truce was drawing near, when, amongst other preparations made to repel the attacks of the Moors, Admiral Herbert, commanding the Mediterranean fleet, put ashore 600 seamen under the command of Captain Barclay, an experienced soldier, who acted as major, and on the 12th September, three troops of cavalry, strong, together with stores and provisions, arrived in the colony at a most opportune moment, as the Moors affirmed that the truce expired on the 15th of that month. The governor replied that this declaration of war on the part of the Moors could not have come at a more seasonable opportunity, as he was thoroughly prepared for defence; but he conceived that the object of the four months' truce, which was now expiring, had been for the purpose of procuring a more lasting peace. Notwithstanding these endeavours of Sir Palmes Fairburn to prolong the truce, the enemy, on the night of the 14th September, removed the poles that marked the boundaries, and on the morning of the 15th commenced firing several shots at the town, which were returned by the garrison.

The Guards had soon an opportunity of meeting their new foe, for in consequence of this threatening attitude of the Moors it was deemed advisable on the 19th September to attack them, and orders

HENRIETTA
FORT

PETERBOROUGH
TOWER
UPPER CASTLE

CHARLES
FORT

TANG

ANN'S
FORT

JAMES
FORT

KATE
FORT

TANGEL
FORT

VOLUNTEERS

DOUGLAS

AFFAIR WITH THE MOORS
AT
TANGIERS.
20ᵗʰ Sepᵗ 1680.

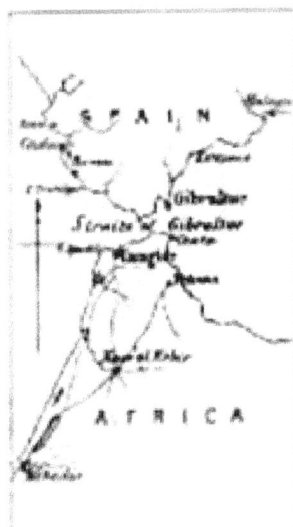

YORK CAS-

PARADE

MER.

IRE

B A Y

EASTERN TOWER

DEVILS TOWER

OLD GATE

OF

IRISH BATTERY

T A N G I E R S.

EAMEN

Bd Corner

S P A I N

Gibraltar

Straits of Gibraltar

Tangier

A F R I C A

Scale of Yards

were given to the whole garrison, now reinforced by the new arrivals, to be under arms by three the following morning. At the appointed hour the troops were at their allotted posts, and shortly afterwards the governor, the admiral. Colonel Sackville, and Colonel Halket arrived on the ground. The English horse were drawn up near Katharina Port, and next to them the advanced guard, composed of all the volunteers and detachments from every battalion, under Colonel Tollemache and Captain Lockart. The King's Battalion, with the Foot Guards, followed, under Captain Bowes of the first regiment; then came Dumbarton's Scots regiment, under Halket, followed by the battalion of seamen. Colonel Sackville, on riding up to the King's Battalion, spoke to them some inspiriting words before going into action, addressing them as "My good fellows."

He told them that as Guardsmen much was expected from them; that they were to act courageously like the King of England's Guards, in a manner worthy of themselves, and that they must show to the world they were worthy of being what they were. He cautioned them against advancing out of the ranks, however much tempted they might be by the enemy to do so; he recommended them to stand well together, to keep close, according to order, and to obey strictly the orders of their officer. He doubted not but that they would overcome the rude and undisciplined attacks of the enemy, gain for themselves the favour of the king and the love of their country, as well as secure to themselves a glorious and everlasting fame, and the good repute of all persons. Colonel Halket also addressed some words to his battalion of Dumbarton's regiment.

About five in the morning, all being ready, the troops marched out at Katharina Port, and almost before the Moorish sentinels could give the alarm of the approach of the Christians, these had formed in order of battle upon advantageous ground, to strengthen which, materials were ordered up from Katharina Port, to make a lodgement, where-upon the Moors came hurrying down the hill in an irregular manner to interrupt its progress. They were received by the advanced guard, under Tollemache, and driven back, when they sought for shelter in the trenches of some old forts, where they were kept in check.

In the meantime strong detachments from the King's Battalion, and from the governor's regiment, were detached to Anne's Fort and Tindal Fort, with orders to drive the enemy back at those points, and to prevent their approaching too near the working parties. The two battalions of Douglas on their left, and of the seamen on the left of all, at a place called Pye Corner, also advanced, charging the enemy and driving them from trench to trench, as far as Portugal Cross, about a mile in advance. The conflict continued for seven or eight hours, and the musketeers of the several battalions emptied three or four collars of bandoliers in the course of these attacks. About two in the afternoon the Moors ceased firing, which enabled the working parties to continue their work at the stockade, and about eight in the evening the several advanced detachments were called in to their respective battalions. The stockade being roughly finished, the King's Battalion, with the advanced guard, were ordered to occupy it that night, the rest of the troops retiring into the town, with the exception of Douglas's battalion, which was left as a reserve outside Katharina Port.

The following morning, the 21st, the troops again took up the same position, and drove the Moors from the trenches, to enable the working party to continue the construction of the wooden fort. This system was continued daily till the work was completed, the troops taking it in turn to occupy the different posts.

On the 21st of September, a detachment of the King's Battalion and of the governor's regiment was again ordered to Anne's Fort, where it gallantly drove the enemy from a trench four or five miles beyond. The governor, writing home on the 23rd September, adds, that Colonel Sackville had proved himself a man of valour and experience, as had also Tollemache, Kirk, and others. After eight days' labour, the fort was finished, 28th September, and a guard of 600 men was left in it, to be relieved every twenty-four hours. The Moors now several times attempted to storm the stockade, but finding their efforts ineffectual, they commenced, as was believed, to undermine it. The governor, apprehensive that such was the case, rode out with his staff to make a reconnaissance, when he received a mortal wound, of which he died at the end of the following month, but being at the time incapacitated from further active service, Lieutenant-Colonel Edward Sackville, as the next senior office at once took upon himself the duties of governor and commander-in-chief.

Various small affairs were constantly occurring with the enemy during the following month, when on the 26th October, it was determined, at a council of war, to attack the Moors in their trenches the following day. Colonel Sackville made all the necessary dispositions, and at three in the morning of the 27th all the troops were at their allotted posts. The action soon began with great spirit on both sides; the English were assisted by the guns from the fleet, and as each trench was carried from the enemy, a British cheer was heard above the din of arms. The King's Battalion, posted on the right of the line, charged and drove back the Moors from the ground whereon they had planted their guns, of which two were captured by them, and Captain Bowes, who was in command of the King's Battalion, considering he had orders to maintain the post he had gained, did not afterwards, though strongly urged by his officer, move to the support of the Scots, but ordered his men to stand to their posts on pain of death. The English and Spanish horse charged the Moorish cavalry wherever they could meet them, and the Moors were eventually driven off the field at all points, with the loss of 600 men killed; and three guns, of which two were captured by the King's Battalion, and of four colours. The number of their wounded uncertain.

The English did not exceed 3000 in number in the action; the Moors were between 15,000 and 16,000 men. During the late operations, from the 20th of September to the 27th October, the loss in killed and wounded on the Christian side was between 600 and 700; that of the Moors, not less than 2000. Of the King's Battalion, Lieutenant Robinson, of the King's Regiment of Guards, was shot through the arm and body, and seven private soldiers were killed and fifty-one wounded. Colonel Sackville was again reported to have distinguished himself, and to have shown good qualities as a general officer.

As many of the enemy's dead were left lying unburied outside the British lines, Colonel Sackville wrote to the Alcade of Tetuan, giving him permission to carry them off, and at the same time apologised to him for the ill-usage they had met with, for all their heads had been cut off; some British soldiers having, on former occasions, been thus treated, no orders to the contrary could prevent their comrades retaliating. The Moors accepted the offer as well as the apology, and brought with them the bodies of three English soldiers that had fallen in their part of the field.

Sir Palmes Fairburn lived to hear the successful result of this last action, and died on the 27th October. One of his last acts while lying on his death-bed was connected with the trial and punishment of an officer of the King's Battalion for killing another, as referred to in his despatch of the 18th of October to the principal Secretary of State, from which it appears that Lieutenant Collier, of the King's Battalion killed Lieutenant Church, of Colonel Sackville's company; Collier was tried by a jury, and, being found guilty of manslaughter, was sentenced to be burnt in the hand, which sentence was carried out.

As, however, he was a very good officer, and the court, after passing sentence, had recommended him to mercy, the governor had seen fit to retain him in his command till the king's pleasure was known; and he was subsequently promoted.

Colonel Sackville despatched Tollemache of the Coldstreams to England at the beginning of December with an account of their late successes: he announced the death of Sir Palmes Fairburn, and requested that the vacancies caused by the late numerous casualties might be filled by volunteers and others then serving at Tangiers, whose names would be shortly forwarded to England. He concludes thus:—

> I pray your lordship to forgive the failings I may commit whilst I have the honour to command here, being truly conscious of every defect but that of my loyalty and religious zeal to serve his majesty, which I shall likewise earnestly labour to express on all occasions of service to Your Lordship, whose favour and protection is needful as it is coveted by,
>
> May it please your lordship,
> Your lordship's
> Most devoted, most obedient, and
> Most humble servant,
> E. Sackville.

A truce was now made for six months, between Colonel Sackville and the *alcade*, and the inhabitants began at once to feel its good effects, provisions of all sorts being brought in by the Moors, who were equally pleased at the turn affairs had taken. A peace was also concluded on the 26th November (though it awaited the king's ratification) between Colonel Sackville and the Alcade of Alcassar, in the name of the Emperor of Morocco. Colonel Sackville, in announcing this event to the Earl of Sunderland, in a letter of the 5th of December, says that as to obtaining the sanction of the Moors, by treaty, to constructing forts outside the town, they would never consent to such a thing so long as a Moor remained alive in Africa.

He adds that the expense of building them would be enormous, and that it would be impossible to hold them permanently when built with less than 10,000 foot and 800 or 1000 cavalry. He refers also to the possibility of his being retained in his present post in succession to Sir Palmes Fairburn. Colonel Sackville, at the same time, addressed a letter to Charles II., explaining the conditions of the treaty, and expressing a hope that he had acted therein according to the king's wishes.

On the reception in England of the news of the late events, Charles sent out Sir James Leslie as his ambassador to the Emperor of Morocco. Sir James arrived at Tangiers on the, and, on being made acquainted with the terms of Colonel Sackville's treaty, he at once objected to ratify it, and, after a long conference with the colonel, he called upon him to give his reasons in writing, for signing the treaty in question, and for considering any delay in its ratification to be dangerous.

Colonel Sackville, in his lengthy reply, 29th of December, stated that he had in mind the king's circumstances at home, that there were but 1500 men fit for duty, and that the maintenance of the war was beyond what the revenues of the Crown could afford; that he had gained better terms than his predecessors did when all the forts were still standing; that to continue the war, more materials (which were not forthcoming) would be required to construct new works; that the *alcade* had declared they would as soon part with their religion as with ground to enable the Christians to fortify upon; and that though Sir James found fault with the terms, he (Colonel Sackville) prided himself more on his success in gaining them than on his successes in the field; and he concluded by criticising the manner in which Sir James had opened his diplomatic intercourse with the *alcade*.

On the 15th of January, 1681, Colonel Sackville also wrote to Lord Sunderland, explaining that he had no ill-will against Sir James Leslie, and that what he had said and done, had been done as most advantageous in his opinion for the king's interest. He denied having any personal interest in the affair whatever, and concluded by saying, as for himself, nothing would give him more pleasure than to be relieved from his present duties and be allowed to return home, making over the command of the troops and his government to whomever his majesty might be pleased to appoint.

Not only did Colonel Sackville differ widely with Sir James Leslie as to the terms of the above treaty, but he had frequent causes of complaint against Admiral Herbert, of whom, in an official despatch of the 11th of February, 1681, to the Earl of Sunderland, he thus expresses himself:

> From whose insupportable and irregular behaviour we have great reliance your lordship will send us your helping hand for our deliverance; for truly, my lord, he is become such a grievance both at sea and on shore that (as I have already acquainted Your Lordship), I despair of any prosperity or success to his

majesty's affairs whilst he has any influence here.

Colonel Sackville was much gratified, in the month of February, by receiving a letter from the Secretary of State, informing him how extremely acceptable the truce was to the king and council. Colonel Kirk had been despatched to the Emperor of Morocco before Sir James Leslie's arrival, and was well received by him; he told Colonel Kirk that for his sake, as he had come to wait upon him, he would give him four years' peace in Tangiers, and he swore by *Allah* that, as long as Colonel Sackville was governor, he would cut off the *alcade's* head if he presumed to break the treaty.

Sir James Leslie proceeded on his embassy to the Emperor of Morocco, on the 9th of March, and finding that he could gain no better terms than those previously agreed to by Colonel Sackville, he eventually, on the 29th of that month, at Mequeness, signed and ratified the treaty, with very slight alterations, and agreed with the emperor that it should continue for four years. No new fortifications were to be built, but those in existence might be kept in a state of repair. Sir James's excuse for not procuring better terms from the emperor than those he found fault with Sackville for having agreed to with the *alcade*, was, that both Colonel Sackville and Colonel Kirk represented to him that the garrison was not in a condition for war.

The request of Colonel Sackville to be relieved was now May 4. granted; he left Tangiers on the 4th of May, and returned to England, and Colonel Kirk was appointed governor in his place, and the detachments of the King's Regiment of Foot Guards, and of the Coldstreams, continued for the time at Tangiers, forming part of the King's Battalion.

Nothing particular occurred in the regiments at home in the year 1680, beyond sending out the above detachments to Tangiers, while the usual reliefs of companies took place at Windsor, Tilbury Fort, and the Tower of London.

![LEONAUR]

ALSO FROM LEONAUR

AVAILABLE IN SOFTCOVER OR HARDCOVER WITH DUST JACKET

THE ART OF WAR *by Antoine Henri Jomini*—Strategy & Tactics From the Age of Horse & Musket.

THE ART OF WAR *by Sun Tzu and Pierre G. T. Beauregard*—*The Art of War* by Sun Tzu and *Principles and Maxims of the Art of War* by Pierre G. T. Beauregard.

THE MILITARY RELIGIOUS ORDERS OF THE MIDDLE AGES *by F. C. Woodhouse*—The Knights Templar, Hospitaller and Others.

THE BENGAL NATIVE ARMY *by F. G. Cardew*—An Invaluable Reference Resource.

ARTILLERY THROUGH THE AGES—*by Albert Manucy*—A History of the DEvelopment and Use of Cannons, Mortars, Rockets & Projectiles from Earliest Times to the Nineteenth Century.

THE SWORD OF THE CROWN *by Eric W. Sheppard*—A History of the British Army to 1914.

THE 7TH (QUEEN'S OWN) HUSSARS: Volume 3—1818-1914 *by C. R. B. Barrett*—On Campaign During the Canadian Rebellion, the Indian Mutiny, the Sudan, Matabeleland, Mashonaland and the Boer War Volume 3: 1818-1914.

THE CAMPAIGN OF WATERLOO *by Antoine Henri Jomini*—A Political & Military History from the French perspective.

RIFLE & DRILL *by S. Bertram Browne*—The Enfield Rifle Musket, 1853 and the Drill of the British Soldier of the Mid-Victorian Period *A Companion to the New Rifle Musket* and *A Practical Guide to Squad and Setting-up Dtill.*

NAPOLEON'S MEN AND METHODS *by Alexander L. Kielland*—The Rise and Fall of the Emperor and His Men Who Fought by His Side.

THE WOMAN IN BATTLE *by Loreta Janeta Velazquez*—Soldier, Spy and Secret Service Agent for the Confederancy During the American Civil War.

THE BATTLE OF ORISKANY 1777 *by Ellis H. Roberts*—The Conflict for the Mowhawk Valley During the American War of Independenc.

PERSONAL RECOLLECTIONS OF JOAN OF ARC *by Mark Twain.*

CAESAR'S ARMY *by Harry Pratt Judson*—The Evolution, Composition, Tactics, Equipment & Battles of the Roman Army.

FREDERICK THE GREAT & THE SEVEN YEARS' WAR *by F. W. Longman.*

LEONAUR

ALSO FROM LEONAUR
AVAILABLE IN SOFTCOVER OR HARDCOVER WITH DUST JACKET

OFFICERS & GENTLEMEN by *Peter Hawker & William Graham*—Two Accounts of British Officers During the Peninsula War: Officer of Light Dragoons by Peter Hawker & Campaign in Portugal and Spain by William Graham .

THE WALCHEREN EXPEDITION by *Anonymous*—The Experiences of a British Officer of the 81st Regt. During the Campaign in the Low Countries of 1809.

LADIES OF WATERLOO by *Charlotte A. Eaton, Magdalene de Lancey & Juana Smith*—The Experiences of Three Women During the Campaign of 1815: Waterloo Days by Charlotte A. Eaton, A Week at Waterloo by Magdalene de Lancey & Juana's Story by Juana Smith.

JOURNAL OF AN OFFICER IN THE KING'S GERMAN LEGION by *John Frederick Hering*—Recollections of Campaigning During the Napoleonic Wars.

JOURNAL OF AN ARMY SURGEON IN THE PENINSULAR WAR by *Charles Boutflower*—The Recollections of a British Army Medical Man on Campaign During the Napoleonic Wars.

ON CAMPAIGN WITH MOORE AND WELLINGTON by *Anthony Hamilton*—The Experiences of a Soldier of the 43rd Regiment During the Peninsular War.

THE ROAD TO AUSTERLITZ by *R. G. Burton*—Napoleon's Campaign of 1805.

SOLDIERS OF NAPOLEON by *A. J. Doisy De Villargennes & Arthur Chuquet*—The Experiences of the Men of the French First Empire: Under the Eagles by A. J. Doisy De Villargennes & Voices of 1812 by Arthur Chuquet .

INVASION OF FRANCE, 1814 by *F. W. O. Maycock*—The Final Battles of the Napoleonic First Empire.

LEIPZIG—A CONFLICT OF TITANS by *Frederic Shoberl*—A Personal Experience of the 'Battle of the Nations' During the Napoleonic Wars, October 14th-19th, 1813.

SLASHERS by *Charles Cadell*—The Campaigns of the 28th Regiment of Foot During the Napoleonic Wars by a Serving Officer.

BATTLE IMPERIAL by *Charles William Vane*—The Campaigns in Germany & France for the Defeat of Napoleon 1813-1814.

SWIFT & BOLD by *Gibbes Rigaud*—The 60th Rifles During the Peninsula War.